4A

PRIMARY MATHEMATICS Standards Edition

TEXTBOOK

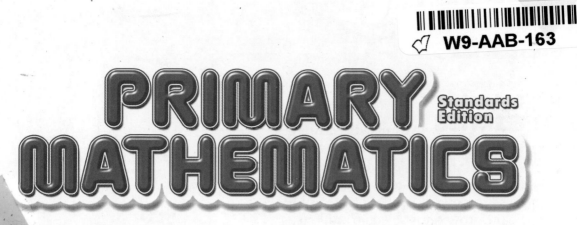

mc Marshall Cavendish Education

SM Singapore Math Inc®

PREFACE

PRIMARY MATHEMATICS (Standards Edition)
is a complete program from the publishers of
Singapore's successful *Primary Mathematics*
series. Newly adapted to align with the
Mathematics Framework for California Public
Schools, the program aims to equip students
with sound concept development, critical
thinking and efficient problem-solving skills.

Mathematical concepts are introduced in the
opening pages and taught to mastery through
specific learning tasks that allow for immediate
assessment and consolidation.

The **modeling method** enables
students to visualize and solve
mathematical problems quickly
and efficiently.

The **Concrete → Pictorial → Abstract**
approach enables students to encounter
math in a meaningful way and translate
mathematical skills from the concrete to
the abstract.

The **pencil icon** [Exercise 18, pages 18–20] provides quick and easy
reference from the Textbook to the relevant Workbook pages.
The **direct correlation** of the Workbook to the Textbook
facilitates focused review and evaluation.

New mathematical concepts are introduced through a **spiral progression** that builds on concepts already taught and mastered.

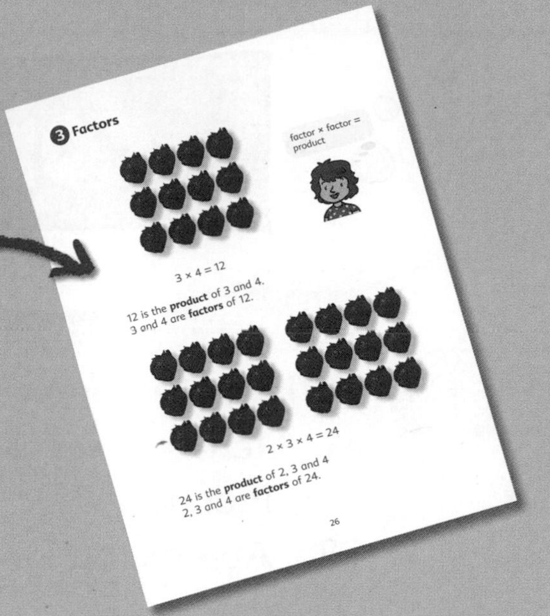

3 Factors

factor × factor = product

$3 \times 4 = 12$

12 is the **product** of 3 and 4.
3 and 4 are **factors** of 12.

$2 \times 3 \times 4 = 24$

24 is the **product** of 2, 3 and 4.
2, 3 and 4 are **factors** of 24.

26

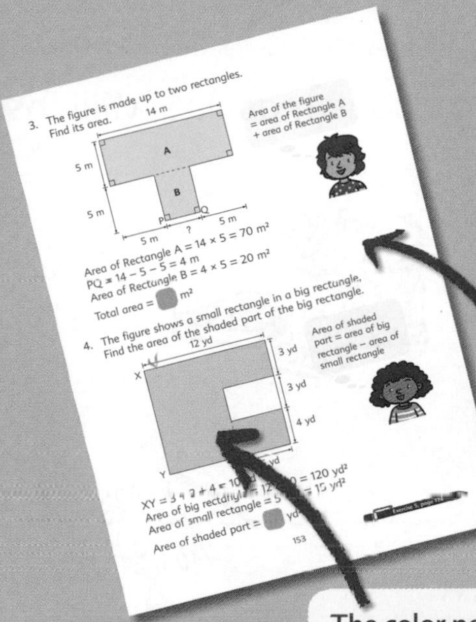

3. The figure is made up to two rectangles. Find its area.

14 m

A

5 m

B

5 m

5 m   P   ?   Q   5 m

Area of the figure = area of Rectangle A + area of Rectangle B

Area of Rectangle A = 14 × 5 = 70 m²
PQ = 14 − 5 − 5 = 4 m
Area of Rectangle B = 4 × 5 = 20 m²

Total area = ⬜ m²

4. The figure shows a small rectangle in a big rectangle. Find the area of the shaded part of the big rectangle.

12 yd

X

3 yd

3 yd

4 yd

Y

Area of shaded part = area of big rectangle − area of small rectangle

XY = 3 + 2 + 4 = 10 ... 12 = 120 yd²
Area of big rectangle = 120 yd²
Area of small rectangle = 5 ... = 15 yd²

Area of shaded part = ⬜ yd²

153

Metacognition is employed as a strategy for learners to monitor their thinking processes in problem solving. Speech and thought bubbles provide guidance through the thought processes, making even the most challenging problems accessible to students.

The color patch ⬜ is used to invite active student participation and to facilitate lively discussion about the mathematical concepts taught.

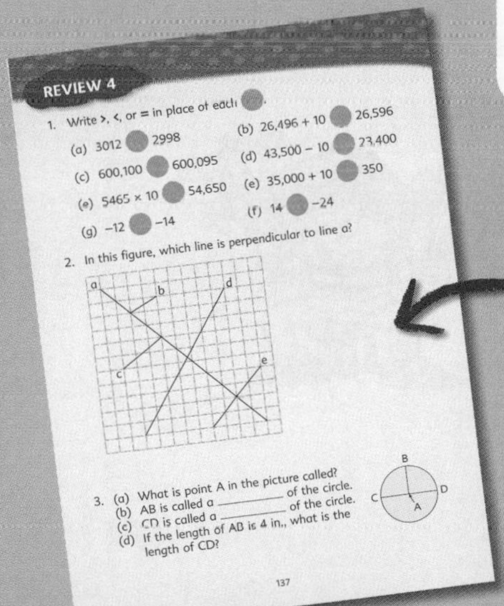

REVIEW 4

1. Write >, <, or = in place of each ⬜.
   (a) 3012 ⬜ 2998
   (b) 26,496 + 10 ⬜ 26,596
   (c) 600,100 ⬜ 600,095
   (d) 43,500 − 10 ⬜ 23,400
   (e) 5465 × 10 ⬜ 54,650
   (e) 35,000 + 10 ⬜ 350
   (g) −12 ⬜ −14
   (f) 14 ⬜ −24

2. In this figure, which line is perpendicular to line a?

   a   b   d

   c   e

3. (a) What is point A in the picture called?
   (b) AB is called a _____ of the circle.
   (c) CD is called a _____ of the circle.
   (d) If the length of AB is 4 in., what is the length of CD?

   B
   C   A   D

137

Regular **reviews** in the Textbook provide consolidation of concepts learned.

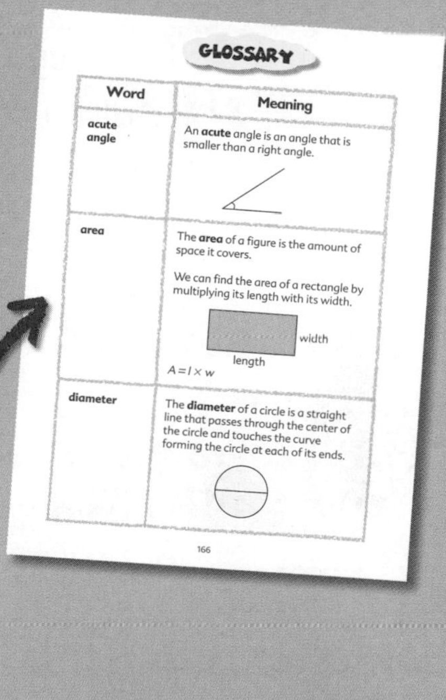

GLOSSARY

Word	Meaning
acute angle	An **acute** angle is an angle that is smaller than a right angle.
area	The **area** of a figure is the amount of space it covers. We can find the area of a rectangle by multiplying its length with its width. width length $A = l \times w$
diameter	The **diameter** of a circle is a straight line that passes through the center of the circle and touches the curve forming the circle at each of its ends.

166

The **glossary** effectively combines pictorial representation with simple mathematical definitions to provide a comprehensive reference guide for students.

CONTENTS

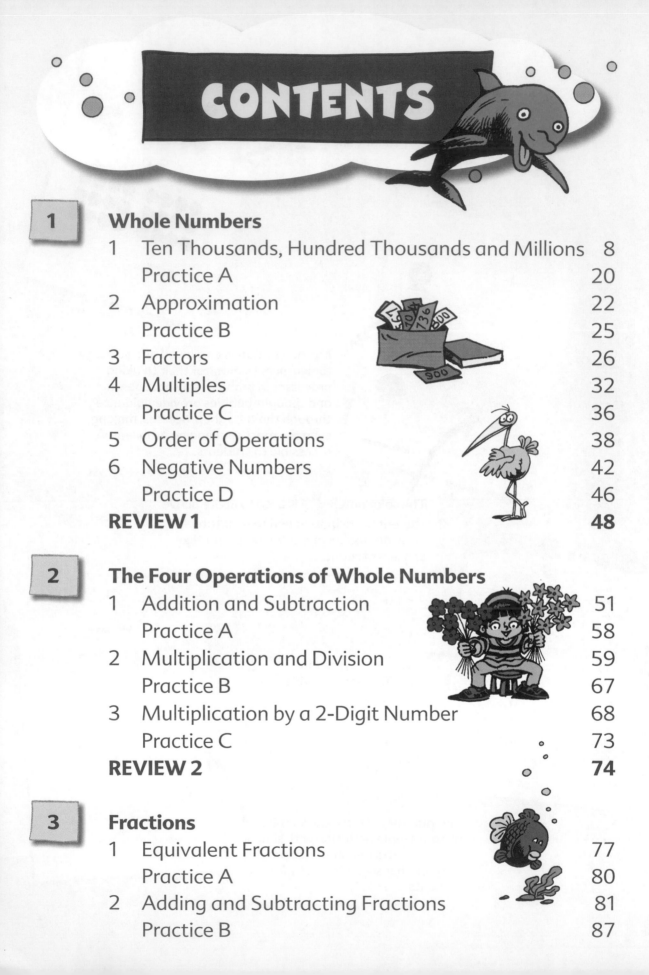

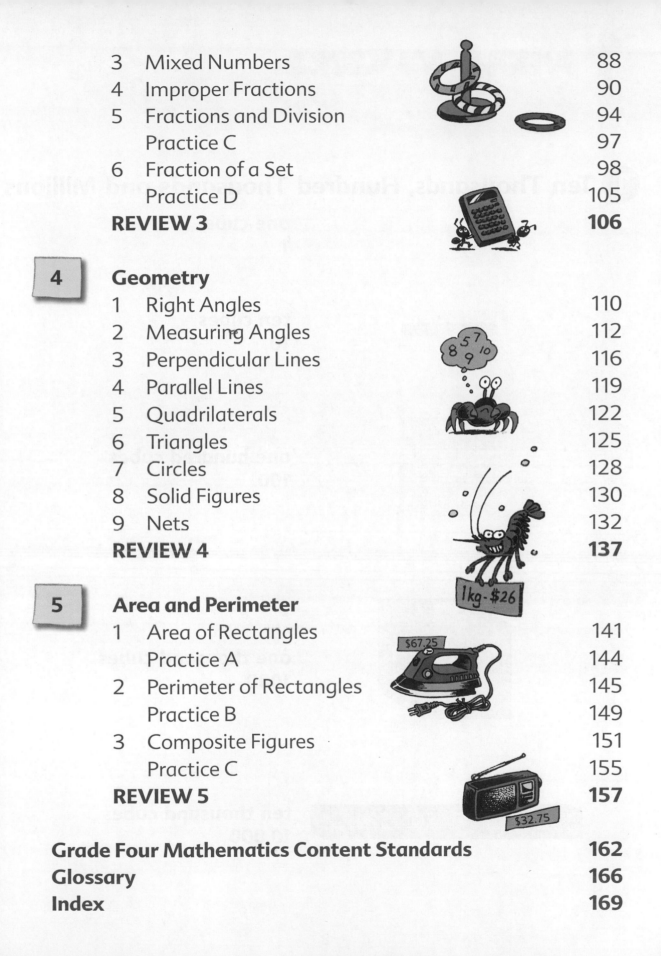

1 WHOLE NUMBERS

1 Ten Thousands, Hundred Thousands and Millions

one cube
1

ten cubes
10

one hundred cubes
100

one thousand cubes
1000

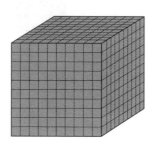

ten thousand cubes
10,000

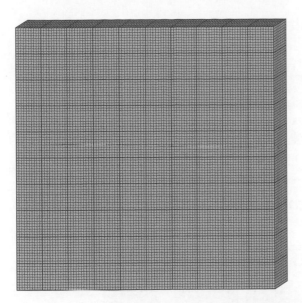

**one hundred thousand cubes
100,000**

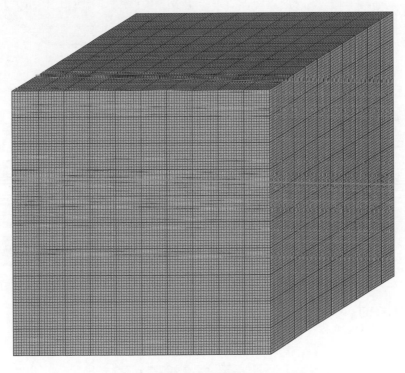

**one million cubes
1,000,000**

one million = a thousand thousands!

1. How many cubes are there altogether?

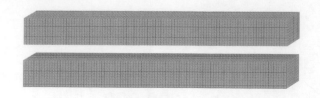

20,000
twenty thousand

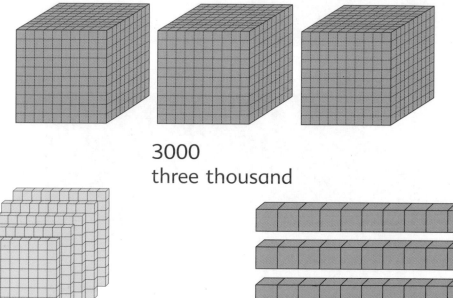

3000
three thousand

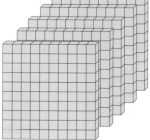

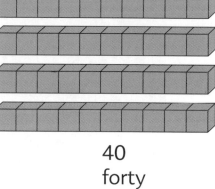

500
five hundred

40
forty

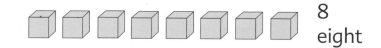
8
eight

The total number of cubes is 23,548.

23,548 is the **standard form** for twenty-three thousand, five hundred forty-eight.

2.

Ten thousands	Thousands	Hundreds	Tens	Ones
10000 10000	1000 1000 1000	100 100 100 100 100	10 10 10 10	1 1 1 1 1 1
2	3	5	4	6

23,546 = 20,000 + 3000 + 500 + 40 + 6
23,546 = 23,000 + 546
twenty-three thousand, five hundred forty-six

20,000 + 3000 + 500 + 40 + 6 is the **expanded form** of 23,546.

23,546 = [2] ten thousands [3] thousands [5] hundreds

[4] tens [6] ones

3. (a) 48,300 = 48 thousands, [3] hundreds

   (b) 60,004 = 60 thousands, [4] ones

4. Write the following in standard form.

   (a) 20 thousands, 8 hundreds = 20,800
   (b) 35 thousands, 6 tens 2 ones = 35,062
   (c) 88 thousands, 7 tens = 88,070
   (d) 70 thousands, 3 ones = 70,003
   (e) 80,000 + 4000 + 90 = 80,490

11

5. A library has a collection of 124,936 books.

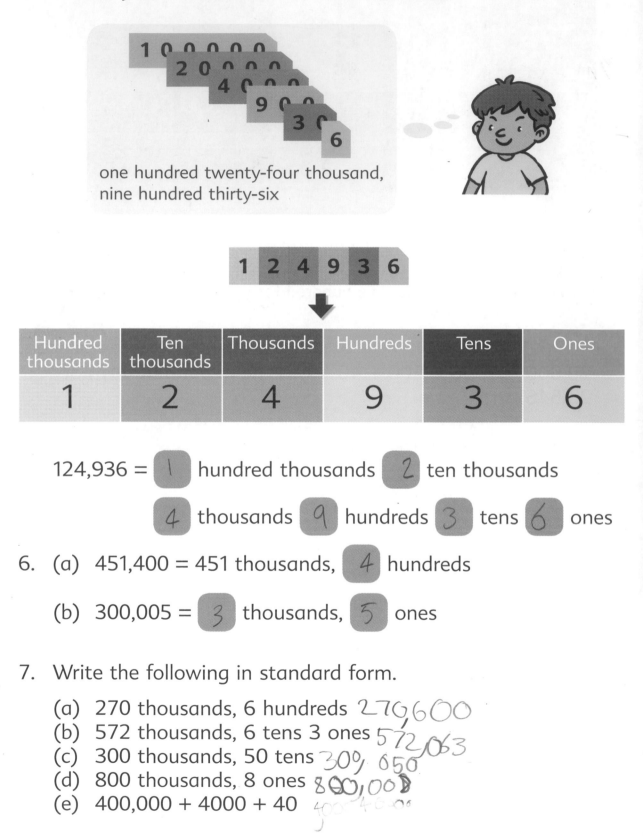

one hundred twenty-four thousand, nine hundred thirty-six

Hundred thousands	Ten thousands	Thousands	Hundreds	Tens	Ones
1	2	4	9	3	6

124,936 = 1 hundred thousands 2 ten thousands

4 thousands 9 hundreds 3 tens 6 ones

6. (a) 451,400 = 451 thousands, 4 hundreds

   (b) 300,005 = 3 thousands, 5 ones

7. Write the following in standard form.

   (a) 270 thousands, 6 hundreds 270,600
   (b) 572 thousands, 6 tens 3 ones 572,063
   (c) 300 thousands, 50 tens 300,050
   (d) 800 thousands, 8 ones 800,008
   (e) 400,000 + 4000 + 40 404,040

12

8. Write the following in standard form.

   √(a) eight thousand, twelve   8000+12
   √(b) forty-nine thousand, five hundred one 49,000 + 500 + 1
   √(c) seventeen thousand, four   17,000 +4
   √(d) ninety thousand, ninety 90,000+90
   √(e) four hundred one thousand, sixty-two +10
   √(f) nine hundred seventy thousand, five hundred five 970, 505
   √(g) seven hundred thousand, nine 700,009

9. Write the following in words.

   (a) 3096   (b) 7280   (c) 5002
   (d) 27,165   (e) 18,057   (f) 42,605
   (g) 30,003   (h) 60,109   (i) 81,900
   (j) 435,672   (k) 500,500   (l) 404,040
   (m) 840,382   (n) 600,005   (o) 999,999

10. Write 805,620 in expanded form.

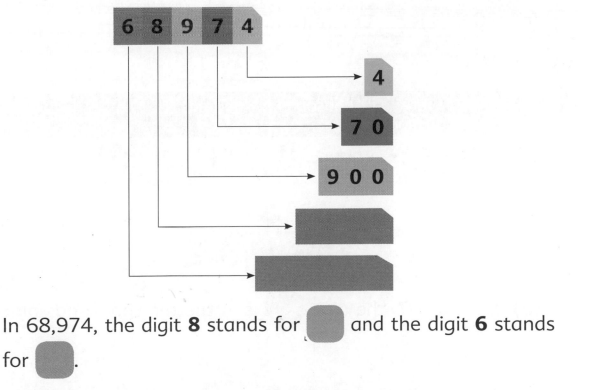

Exercise 1, pages 7-9

11. Use place-value cards to make a 5-digit number like this:

   6 8 9 7 4

   4

   7 0

   9 0 0

   In 68,974, the digit **8** stands for ⬚ and the digit **6** stands
   for ⬚.

13

12. (a) Count the ten thousands, thousands, hundreds, tens and ones in this chart.

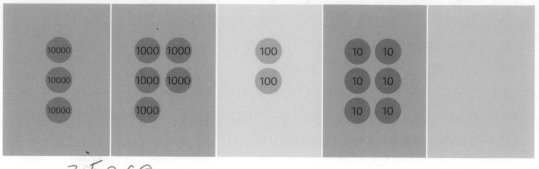

35,260

(b) What number is represented by the set of number discs?
(c) Which digit is in the hundreds place? 2
(d) Which digit is in the ten thousands place? 3
(e) What is the value of each digit in the number?

13. 26,345 people watched a soccer game at a stadium.

(a) Use a set of number discs to represent 26,345.

(b) 26,345 is 345 more than 26,000.

(c) 26,345 is 20,000 more than 6345.

14.

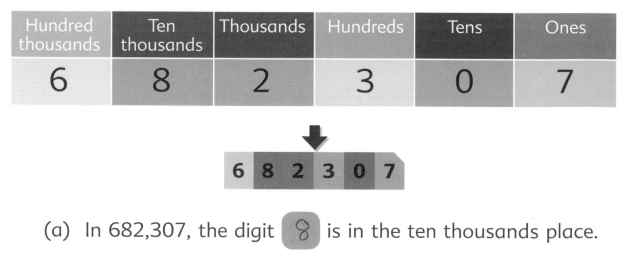

Hundred thousands	Ten thousands	Thousands	Hundreds	Tens	Ones
6	8	2	3	0	7

6 8 2 3 0 7

(a) In 682,307, the digit 8 is in the ten thousands place.

(b) The digit 6 is in the hundred thousands place. Its value is 600000

(c) The digit 0 in the tens place shows that there are no tens.

(d) 682,307 is 600000 more than 82,307.

15. What does the digit 8 stand for in each of the following numbers?

(a) 16,**8**14   (b) **8**2,114   (c) 4**8**,050
(d) **8**26,042   (e) 92**8**,000   (f) 450,03**8**

Exercise 2, pages 10-12

16. The selling price of the house is $2 million. How many one-thousand-dollar bills do you need to buy the house?

We write $2 million as $2,000,000.

1 million = 1000 thousands
2 million = 2 thousands

In 2,000,000, the digit 2 is in the million place.

15

17. In October of 2006, the population of the United States reached 300,000,000.

    We read 300,000,000 as three hundred million.

    In 300,000,000, the digit **3** is in the hundred millions place.

18. 295,314,786 = 2 hundred millions **9** ten millions

    5 millions 3 hundred thousands

    1 ten thousand 4 thousands

    7 hundreds **8** tens 6 ones

19. Write 430,612,043 in expanded form. 400,000,000 + 30,000,000 600,000 + 10,000 + 2000 + 40 + 3

20. 45,802,109 is 45 million more than 802,109

21. The Sun is about 93,000,000 miles from Earth.

    (a) The digit 9 is in the ten millions place. Its value is 90,000,000.

    (b) The digit 3 is in the millions place.

22. Saturn is about 821,190,000 miles from Earth.

    (a) What digit is in the ten thousands place? 9

    (b) What digit is in the ten millions place? 2

    (c) What value does the digit 8 have in this number? 8 hundred thousand

23. Write the following in standard form.

    (a) six million   600,000,000

    (b) seventy million, three thousand   70,003,000

    (c) forty-two million, eight hundred sixty-one thousand, three

    (d) four hundred twenty million, seventy-two thousand, one hundred thirty

16

24. Write the following in words.

   (a) 5,000,000   (b) 14,126,000
   (c) 90,040,003   (d) 450,125,400

Exercise 3, pages 13-14

25. What are the missing numbers in the regular number patterns in this number puzzle?

5000	6000	7000				
					20,000	
29,500	29,600	29,700				30,100
			28,800			
24,230						
24,130			26,800		60,000	
24,030					70,000	
			24,800			
23,830	23,820	23,810				23,770
23,630		23,650		23,670		23,690

26. (a) What number is 10,000 more than 345,084? 355,084

    (b) What number is 100,000 more than 1,934,006?

    (c) What number is 2000 less than 34,569,203? 34,567,203

    (d) What number is 1,000,000 less than 200,000,000? 199,000,000

    (e) What number is 400 less than 90,000,000? 89,999,600

27. Complete the following regular number patterns.

    (a) 83,002, 93,002, 103,002, 113,002, 123,002

    (b) 4,742,000, 3,742,000, 2,742,000, 1,742,000, 742,000

    (c) 96,000,000, 98,000,000, 100,000,000, 102,000,000, 104,000,000

17

28. What number does each letter represent?

(a)
A   B   C   D   E
5000 *5100* *5300* 5500 *5700* *5900* 6000   *6400*

(b)
P   Q   R   S   T
4900 50,000 *52,000* *54,000* 55,000   *58,000* 60,000 *61,000*

29. (a) Which number is smaller, 56,700 or 75,600?

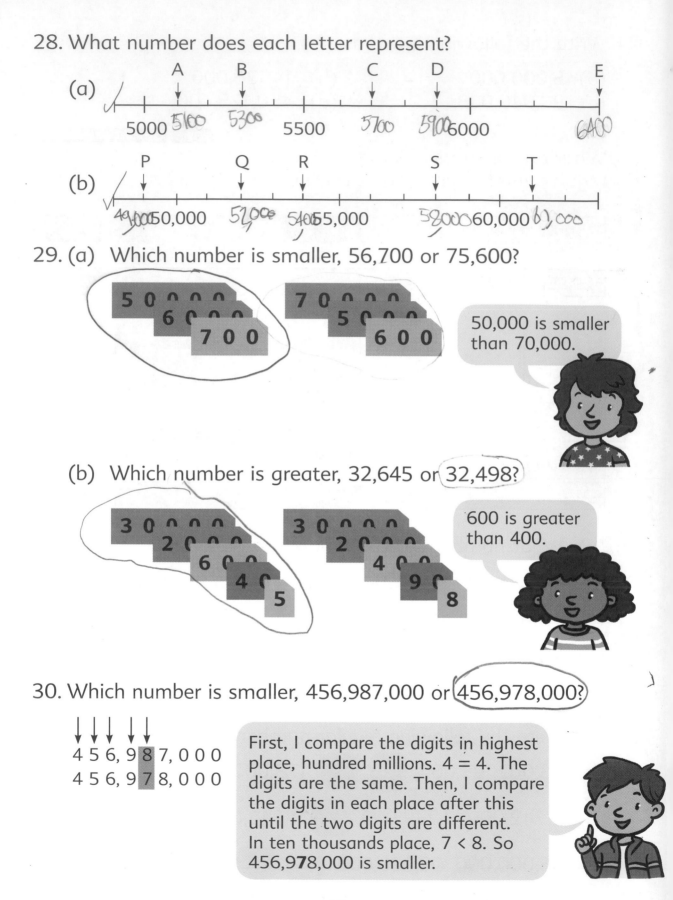

50,000 is smaller than 70,000.

(b) Which number is greater, 32,645 or 32,498?

600 is greater than 400.

30. Which number is smaller, 456,987,000 or 456,978,000?

4 5 6, 9 8 7, 0 0 0
4 5 6, 9 7 8, 0 0 0

First, I compare the digits in highest place, hundred millions. 4 = 4. The digits are the same. Then, I compare the digits in each place after this until the two digits are different. In ten thousands place, 7 < 8. So 456,978,000 is smaller.

18

31. Which number is greater, 95,030 or 154,030?

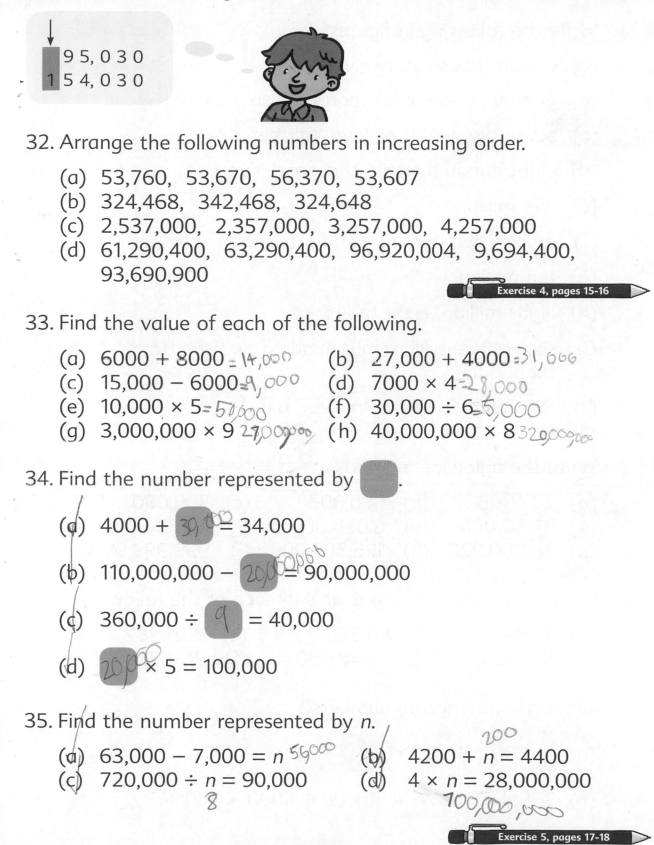

    9 5, 0 3 0
  1 5 4, 0 3 0

32. Arrange the following numbers in increasing order.
   (a) 53,760, 53,670, 56,370, 53,607
   (b) 324,468, 342,468, 324,648
   (c) 2,537,000, 2,357,000, 3,257,000, 4,257,000
   (d) 61,290,400, 63,290,400, 96,920,004, 9,694,400,
       93,690,900

Exercise 4, pages 15-16

33. Find the value of each of the following.
   (a) 6000 + 8000 = 14,000   (b) 27,000 + 4000 = 31,000
   (c) 15,000 − 6000 = 9,000   (d) 7000 × 4 = 28,000
   (e) 10,000 × 5 = 50,000   (f) 30,000 ÷ 6 = 5,000
   (g) 3,000,000 × 9 = 27,000,000 (h) 40,000,000 × 8 = 320,000,000

34. Find the number represented by ▮.

   (a) 4000 + 30,000 = 34,000

   (b) 110,000,000 − 20,000,000 = 90,000,000

   (c) 360,000 ÷ 9 = 40,000

   (d) 20,000 × 5 = 100,000

35. Find the number represented by n.
   (a) 63,000 − 7,000 = n 56,000   (b) 4200 + n = 4400   200
   (c) 720,000 ÷ n = 90,000   8   (d) 4 × n = 28,000,000
                                          100,000,000

Exercise 5, pages 17-18

1. Write the following in figures.

   (a) eleven thousand, twelve

   (b) one hundred fifteen thousand, six hundred

   (c) seven hundred thousand, thirteen

   (d) eight hundred eighty thousand, five

   (e) five million

   (f) four million, two hundred thousand

   (g) ten million

   (h) eight million, eight thousand

   (i) sixty-three million, four hundred two thousand, six hundred

   (j) one hundred twenty million, four thousand, twenty

2. Write the following in words.

   (a) 207,306   (b) 560,003   (c) 700,000
   (d) 3,450,000   (e) 6,020,000   (f) 4,003,000
   (g) 48,000,020 (h) 126,300,000 (i) 999,999,999

3. What is the value of the digit 8 in each of the following?

   (a) 72,**8**45   (b) **8**0,375   (c) 901,9**8**2
   (d) **8**10,034   (e) 9,64**8**,000 (f) **8**,162,000

4. What are the missing numbers?

   (a) $16,500 = 10,000 + \boxed{} + 500$

   (b) $225,430 = \boxed{} + 20,000 + 5000 + 400 + 30$

(c) $100{,}000 + 80{,}000 + 4000 + 900 =$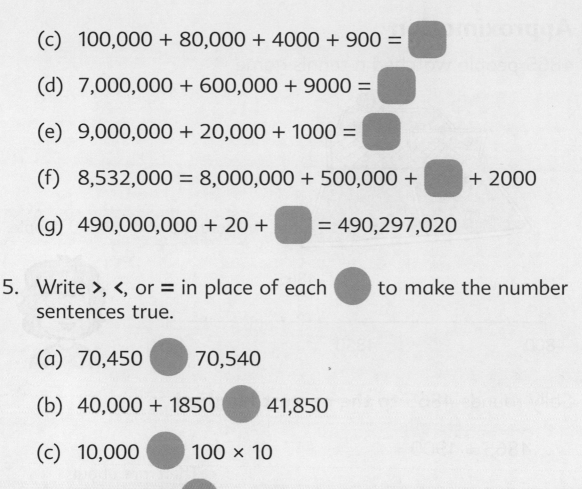

(d) $7{,}000{,}000 + 600{,}000 + 9000 =$

(e) $9{,}000{,}000 + 20{,}000 + 1000 =$

(f) $8{,}532{,}000 = 8{,}000{,}000 + 500{,}000 +$ ⬜ $+ 2000$

(g) $490{,}000{,}000 + 20 +$ ⬜ $= 490{,}297{,}020$

5. Write **>**, **<**, or **=** in place of each ⬤ to make the number sentences true.

(a) $70{,}450$ ⬤ $70{,}540$

(b) $40{,}000 + 1850$ ⬤ $41{,}850$

(c) $10{,}000$ ⬤ 100×10

(d) 80×1000 ⬤ $80{,}000$

(e) $56{,}903$ ⬤ $59{,}609$

6. Find the missing number represented by a.

(a) $400{,}000{,}000 + 80{,}000{,}000 + a = 480{,}100{,}000$

(b) $4600 - a = 600$

(c) $4800 \div a = 600$

(d) $4600 + a = 4800$

(e) $4000 \times a = 32{,}000$

2 Approximation

4865 people watched a tennis game.

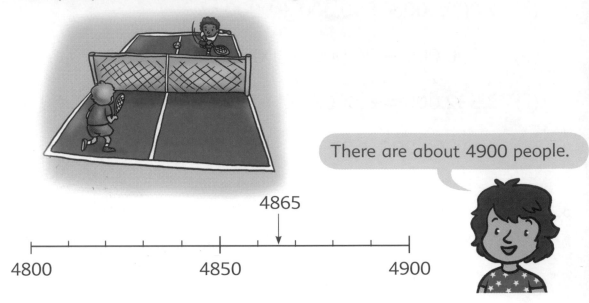

There are about 4900 people.

4865

```
├────┼────┼────┼────┼────┤
4800        4850        4900
```

Sally rounds 4865 **to the nearest hundred**.

$4865 \approx 4900$

4865 is **approximately** 4900.

There are about 5000 people.

4865

```
├───┼───┼───┼───┼───┼───┼───┼───┼───┤
4000          4500          5000
```

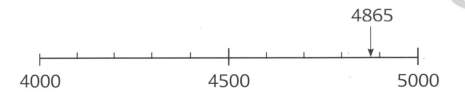

Jenny rounds 4865 **to the nearest thousand**.

$4865 \approx 5000$

4865 is **approximately** 5000.

We use the approximation sign $\approx$ to show rounding of numbers.

1. There are 487 pages in a book.
   Round the number of pages to the nearest ten.

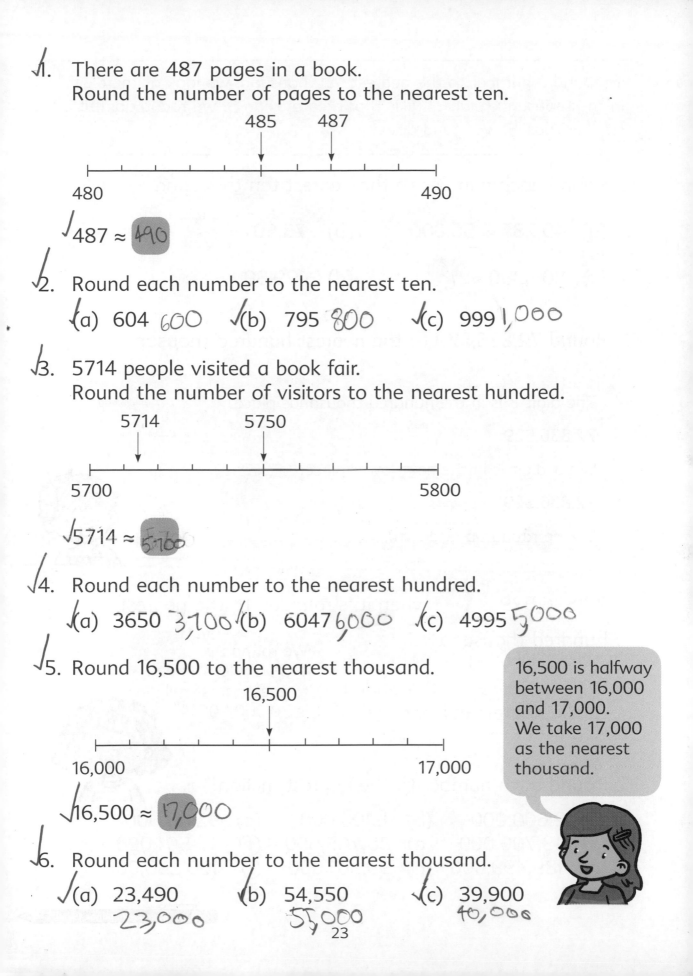

485   487

480   490

487 ≈ **490**

2. Round each number to the nearest ten.
   (a) 604 600   (b) 795 800   (c) 999 1,000

3. 5714 people visited a book fair.
   Round the number of visitors to the nearest hundred.

5714   5750

5700   5800

5714 ≈ **5,700**

4. Round each number to the nearest hundred.
   (a) 3650 3,700 (b) 6047 6,000 (c) 4995 5,000

5. Round 16,500 to the nearest thousand.

16,500

16,000   17,000

16,500 ≈ **17,000**

> 16,500 is halfway between 16,000 and 17,000. We take 17,000 as the nearest thousand.

6. Round each number to the nearest thousand.
   (a) 23,490   (b) 54,550   (c) 39,900
       23,000   55,000   40,000

23

To round a number to the nearest ten thousand, we look at the digit in the thousands place. If it is 5 or greater than 5, we round up. If it is smaller than 5, we round down.

7. Round each number to the nearest ten thousand.

   (a) 49,287 ≈ 50,000   (b) 73,501 ≈ 70,000

   (c) 804,390 ≈ 800,000   (d) 129,500 ≈ 130,000

8. Round 72,836,529 to the nearest hundred thousand.

   The digit 8 is in the hundred thousands place.

   72,**8**36,529

   What digit is in the next lower place?

   72,8**3**6,529

   Do we round up or down?

   72,836,529 is 72,800,000 when it is rounded to the nearest hundred thousand.

9. What is 19,796,030 rounded to the nearest million?   20,000,000

We round up. 19,796,030 rounded to the nearest million is 20,000,000.

10. Round each number to the nearest million.

   (a) 2,600,000   3,000,000   (b) 1,200,000   1,000,000   (c) 9,500,000   10,000,000
   (d) 43,700,000   44,000,000   (e) 38,765,000   39,000,000   (f) 47,501,000   50,000,000
   (g) 189,499,000   189,000,000 (h) 99,501,000   100,000,000   (i) 100,230,000   100,000,000

Exercise 6, pages 19-20

1. Round each number to the nearest ten.

   (a) 72   (b) 655   (c) 1289

2. Round each number to the nearest hundred.

   (a) 342   (b) 1259   (c) 20,753

3. Round each number to the nearest thousand.

   (a) 6850   (b) 10,500   (c) 125,498

4. Round each number to the nearest hundred thousand.

   (a) 8,765,000   (b) 7,561,000   (c) 91,499,000

5. David bought a television set for $849.
   Round this amount to the nearest hundred dollars.

6. Mr. Ray bought a car for $69,500.
   Round this amount to the nearest thousand dollars.

7. A spaceship traveled 999,540 km.
   Round this distance to the nearest thousand km.

8. Round each of the following numbers to the nearest million.
   (a) 6,638,000   (b) 20,702,000
   (c) 156,499,000   (d) 349,750,000

9. In March 2005, about 35,200,000 immigrants were recorded as living in the United States. What place was this number rounded to?

10. A number is rounded to 5,349,000. What are the smallest and greatest possible values for this number?

③ Factors

factor × factor = product

3 × 4 = 12

12 is the **product** of 3 and 4.
3 and 4 are **factors** of 12.

2 × 3 × 4 = 24

24 is the **product** of 2, 3 and 4.
2, 3 and 4 are **factors** of 24.

1.

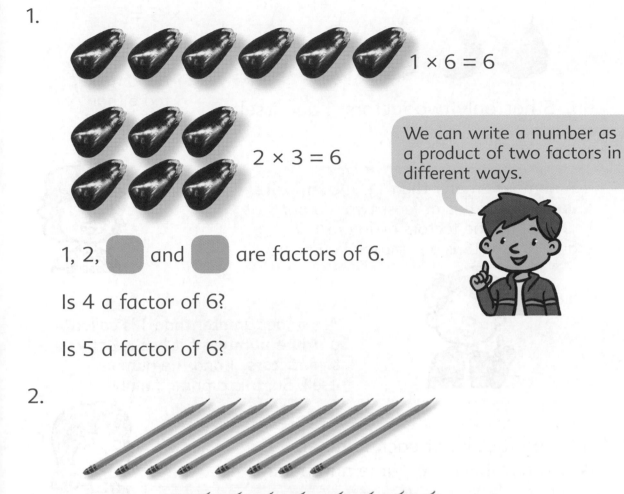

$1 \times 6 = 6$

$2 \times 3 = 6$

We can write a number as a product of two factors in different ways.

1, 2, ⬜ and ⬜ are factors of 6.

Is 4 a factor of 6?

Is 5 a factor of 6?

2.

2 and 8 are factors of 16.
Name other factors of 16.

$2 \times 8 = 16$

⬜ $\times 4 = 16$

3.

$1 \times 5 = 5$

5 has only two factors, 1 and itself, 5.

Can I make more than one equal row?

A number greater than 1 is a **composite number** if it has at least two factors that are not 1. The factors of 16 are 1, 2, 4, 8 and 16. So, 16 is a composite number.

A number greater than 1 is called a **prime number** if it has exactly two factors, 1 and the number itself. So, 5 is a prime number.

4. Find the factors of each number.
    Which numbers are prime numbers?

    (a) 7   (b) 9   (c) 3   (d) 18
    (e) 11   (f) 15   (g) 10   (h) 13

1 is not a prime number or a composite number.

5. (a) Which of the following numbers have 2 as a factor?
        8,   10,   15,   24

    (b) Which of the following numbers have 5 as a factor?
        15,   20,   25,   32

Exercise 7, pages 21-22

6. (a) Is 3 a factor of 21?

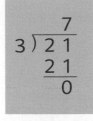

21 can be divided by 3 exactly.
So 3 is a factor of 21.

(b) Is 3 a factor of 26?

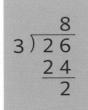

26 cannot be divided by 3 exactly.
So 3 is not a factor of 26.

7. (a) Is 2 a factor of 98?

   (b) Is 4 a factor of 98?

8. (a) Is 4 a factor of 60?

   (b) Is 4 a factor of 84?

   (c) Is 4 a **common factor** of 60 and 84?

9. (a) Is 5 a common factor of 75 and 80?

   (b) Is 8 a common factor of 72 and 96?

10. Find the missing factors.

   (a) $28 = 7 \times$ 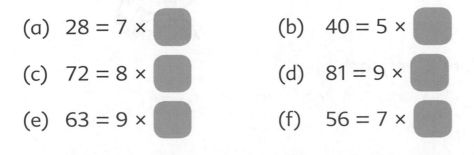   (b) $40 = 5 \times$

   (c) $72 = 8 \times$ (d) $81 = 9 \times$

   (e) $63 = 9 \times$ (f) $56 = 7 \times$

11. Find the factors of 32.

$$32 = 1 \times 32$$
$$32 = 2 \times 16$$
$$32 = 4 \times 8$$

The factors of 32 are 1, 2 ☐ , ☐ , ☐ and ☐ .

12. Find the factors of 48.

$$48 = 1 \times 48$$

$$48 = 2 \times \boxed{}$$

$$48 = 3 \times \boxed{}$$

$$48 = 4 \times \boxed{}$$

$$48 = 6 \times \boxed{}$$

The factors of 48 are 1, 2, 3, 4, 6, ☐ , ☐ , ☐ , ☐ and 48.

13. Find the factors of 100.

$$100 = 1 \times 100$$
$$= 2 \times 50$$
$$= 4 \times 25$$
$$= \ldots$$

14. Find the factors of each number.

(a) 40   (b) 50   (c) 75   (d) 80

15. Find the missing factors.

$12 = 4 \times 3$

$= 2 \times 2 \times 3$

$2 \times 2 \times 3 = 2 \times 3 \times 2$

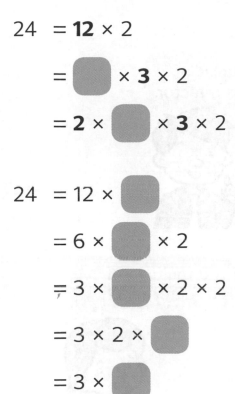

$12 = 6 \times 2$

$= 2 \times \boxed{} \times 2$

$24 = 12 \times 2$

$= \boxed{} \times 3 \times 2$

$= 2 \times \boxed{} \times 3 \times 2$

$24 = 12 \times \boxed{}$

$= 6 \times \boxed{} \times 2$

$= 3 \times \boxed{} \times 2 \times 2$

$= 3 \times 2 \times \boxed{}$

$= 3 \times \boxed{}$

16. Find the missing factors represented by n.

(a) $30 = 5 \times 2 \times n$ (b) $16 = 4 \times n \times 2$
(c) $35 \times 3 = 5 \times n \times 3$ (d) $25 \times 24 = 25 \times 4 \times n$
(e) $4 \times 24 = 8 \times n$ (f) $64 \times 2 = n \times 4$

Exercise 8, pages 23-25
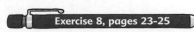

4 Multiples

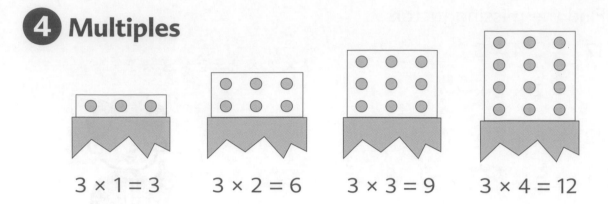

$3 \times 1 = 3$ $3 \times 2 = 6$ $3 \times 3 = 9$ $3 \times 4 = 12$

3, 6, 9 and 12 are **multiples** of 3.

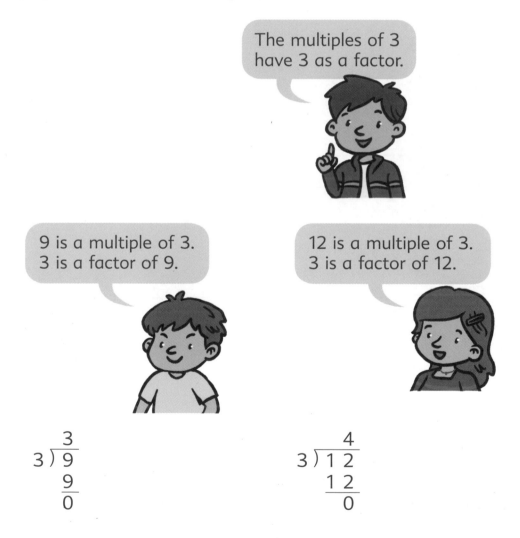

The multiples of 3 have 3 as a factor.

9 is a multiple of 3.
3 is a factor of 9.

12 is a multiple of 3.
3 is a factor of 12.

$$3\overline{)9} \quad \begin{array}{r} 3 \\ \hline 9 \\ 9 \\ \hline 0 \end{array}$$

$$3\overline{)12} \quad \begin{array}{r} 4 \\ \hline 1\,2 \\ 1\,2 \\ \hline 0 \end{array}$$

Name other multiples of 3.

1. (a) Is 3 a factor of 36? yes

    (b) Is 36 a multiple of 3? yes $3 \times 12 = 36$

$$3 \overline{)\begin{array}{l} 1\;2 \\ 3\;6 \\ \end{array}}$$
```
      1 2
   3 ) 3 6
       3
       ---
       6
       6
       ---
       0
```

2. (a) Is 3 a factor of 23? no

    (b) Is 23 a multiple of 3? no

3. (a) Is 12 a multiple of 2? yes

    (b) Is 12 a multiple of 3? yes

    (c) Is 12 a multiple of 4? yes

    (d) Is 12 a multiple of 5? no

    (e) Is 12 a multiple of 6? yes

4. List the first four multiples of 5.

    5,10,15,20

$5 \times 1 = 5$
$5 \times 2 = 10$
$5 \times 3 = 15$
$5 \times 4 = 20$

5. List the first four multiples of 9.   9,18,27,36

6. Find the next three numbers in each of the following regular number patterns.

    (a) 4, 8, 12, 16, 20 , 24 , 28

    (b) 6, 12, 18, 24, 30 , 36 , 42

7. In the table below, the multiples of 2 are circled and the multiples of 5 are crossed.

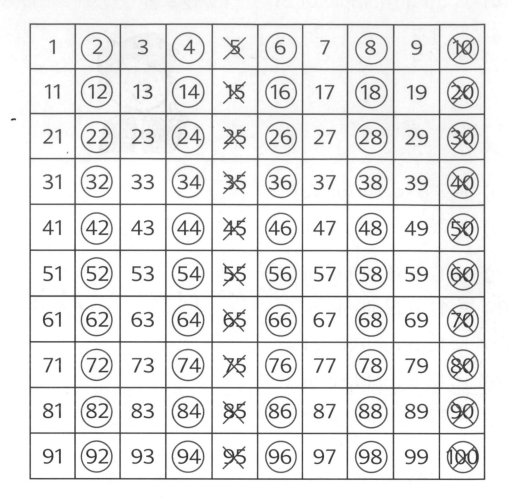

(a) When a number is a multiple of 2, its ones digit is 0, 2, 4 , 6 , or 8 .

(b) When a number is a multiple of 5, its ones digit is 0 , or 5 .

8. Write any number that is a multiple of 3. 18
   Find the sum of the digits of the number. 9
   Is the sum a multiple of 3? yes

9. The multiples of 4 are

    4,   8,   **12**,   16,   20,   24,   28,   ...

    The multiples of 6 are

    6,   **12**,   18,   24,   30,   36,   42,   ...

    12 is a **common multiple** of 4 and 6.

    Name the next two common multiples of 4 and 6. 24, 36

There is more than
one common multiple
of 4 and 6.

10. (a) Which of the following numbers are common factors of
         36 and 63?

    ③   4   ⑥   ⑨   12

    (b) Which of the following numbers are common multiples
         of 6 and 9?

    ⑨   ⑱   27   ㉟   45

11. Find a common multiple of 3 and 5.

The multiples of 5 are
5, 10, 15, 20, ...
15 is also a multiple of 3.

Exercise 9, pages 26-27

PRACTICE C

1. List all the factors of 18.

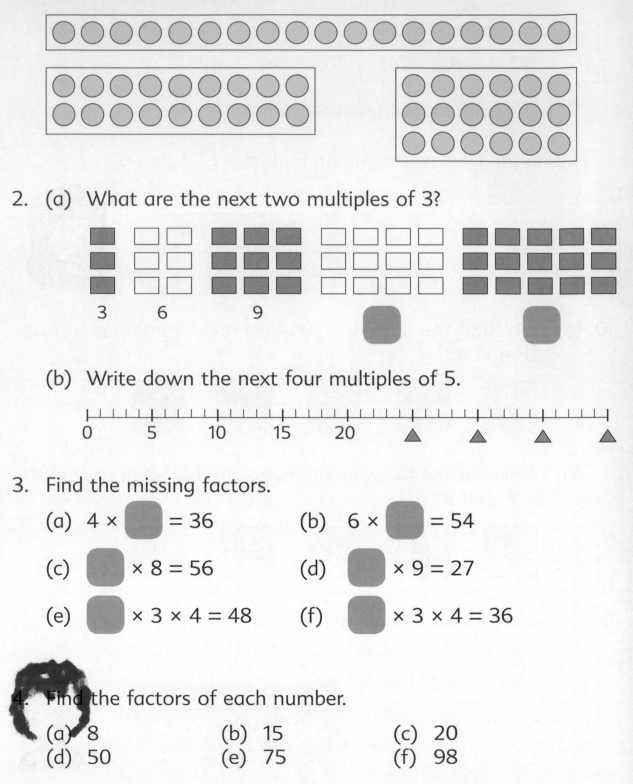

2. (a) What are the next two multiples of 3?

   3   6   9

   (b) Write down the next four multiples of 5.

3. Find the missing factors.

   (a) 4 × ⬜ = 36   (b) 6 × ⬜ = 54

   (c) ⬜ × 8 = 56   (d) ⬜ × 9 = 27

   (e) ⬜ × 3 × 4 = 48   (f) ⬜ × 3 × 4 = 36

4. Find the factors of each number.

   (a) 8   (b) 15   (c) 20
   (d) 50   (e) 75   (f) 98

5. Find a common factor of each pair of numbers.

    (a) 15 and 6   (b) 12 and 16   (c) 15 and 18

6. List the first four multiples of each number.

    (a) 2   (b) 6   (c) 8

7. Find a common multiple of each set of numbers.

    (a) 3 and 4   (b) 4 and 5   (c) 4 and 6

8. Which of the following are prime numbers?

    1, 2, 3, 4, 5, 6, 7, 8, 9, 10

⑤ Order of Operations

Matthew arranges his stamps on two pages of his stamp album like this:

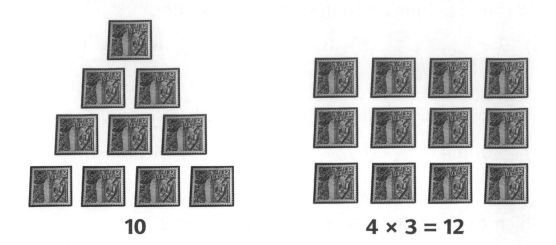

10   **4 × 3 = 12**

Then he finds the total number of stamps.

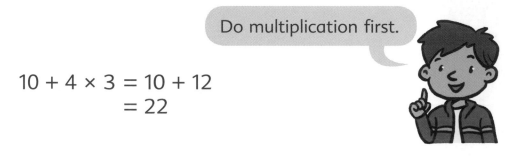

Do multiplication first.

10 + 4 × 3 = 10 + 12
           = 22

There are 22 stamps altogether.

Order of Operations:
Do multiplication or division from left to right, then addition or subtraction from left to right.

1. Find the value of each of the following.
   (a) 12 + 8 − 10
   (b) 60 − 12 − 24
   (c) 31 − 19 + 11
   (d) 43 + 16 − 27
   (e) 64 + 26 + 57
   (f) 90 − 12 + 21
   (g) 15 + 19 − 5
   (h) 61 − 19 − 11
   (i) 58 − 25 + 42

2. Find the value of each of the following.
   (a) 2 × 4 × 8
   (b) 60 ÷ 4 ÷ 3
   (c) 54 ÷ 6 × 3
   (d) 4 × 5 × 6
   (e) 72 ÷ 6 ÷ 4
   (f) 4 × 20 ÷ 8
   (g) 4 × 2 × 20
   (h) 64 ÷ 8 ÷ 8
   (i) 9 × 8 ÷ 9

> An **expression** has numbers and operation signs (+, −, ×, ÷). It does not have an equal sign.

3. Find the value of each expression.
   (a) 9 + 3 × 6
   (b) 27 − 12 ÷ 3
   (c) 4 + 5 × 8
   (d) 80 − 5 × 10
   (e) 54 − 48 ÷ 6
   (f) 9 + 81 ÷ 9
   (g) 56 − 8 × 5 + 4
   (h) 70 + 40 ÷ 5 × 4
   (i) 96 ÷ 8 − 6 × 2
   (j) 6 + 54 ÷ 9 × 2
   (k) 49 − 45 ÷ 5 × 3
   (l) 62 + 42 ÷ 7 − 6

Exercise 10, pages 28-29

4. Find the value of 27 − 2 × (3 + 5).

   27 − 2 × **(3 + 5)**

   = 27 − 2 × **8**

   =

> Do what is in the parentheses first.

5. Find the value of each of the following.
   (a) 9 + (36 + 16)
   (b) 100 − (87 − 13)
   (c) 99 − (87 + 12)
   (d) 18 × (5 × 2)
   (e) 49 ÷ (7 × 7)
   (f) 100 × (27 ÷ 9)

Exercise 11, pages 30-31

6. Find the value of each of the following.

    (a) $60 \div (4 + 8)$ (b) $20 - 2 \times (18 \div 6)$
    (c) $25 + (5 + 7) \div 3$ (d) $(22 + 10) \div 8 \times 5$
    (e) $(50 - 42) \div 2 \times 7$ (f) $100 \div 10 \times (4 + 6)$

7. (a) Shawna had $20. She spent $8 on a toy and $5 on a book. How much money does she have now?

       Shawna spent $8 + $5.

       We can write the expression

       $20 − ($8 + $5)

       Find how much money she had left.

   (b) Paul had $20 and spent $8. He then made $5 more. How much money does he have now?

       We can write the expression

       ($20 − $8) + $5

       How much money does he have now?

   (c) Is $20 − ($8 + $5) the same as ($20 − $8) + $5?

8. Mrs. Harris bought 5 bags of apples and 2 boxes of oranges. There were 8 apples in each bag and 16 oranges in each box.

   (a) Write an expression for how many fruits she bought altogether, using the numbers 2, 5, 8 and 16 only.

   (b) How many fruits did she buy altogether?

An **equation** is a number sentence stating that two amounts are equal.

9. This equation is true.

   $8 = 2 \times 4$

   (a) Add 10 to both sides. Is the equation still true?
   $8 + 10 = (2 \times 4) + 10$

   (b) Add 10 to one side and 2×5 to the other side. Is the equation still true?
   $8 + 10 = (2 \times 4) + (2 \times 5)$

   (c) Multiply both sides by 10. Is the equation still true?
   $8 \times 10 = (2 \times 4) \times 10$

   (d) Multiply one side by 10 and the other side by $(5 + 5)$. Is the equation still true?

   $8 \times 10 = 2 \times 4 \times (5 + 5)$

   If you add or multiply both sides of an equation by the same number, the two sides stay equal.

10. Find the number that goes in the ⬛ to make the equation true.

    (a) $24 + (15 - 4) = \boxed{24} + 11$

    (b) $(4 + 5) \times (3 + 7) = \boxed{9} \times 10$

    (c) $100 \times (10 \div 5) = \boxed{100} \times 2$

    (d) $(14 + 10) \div 2 \times 3 = \boxed{12} \times 3$

Exercise 12, pages 32-33

6 Negative Numbers

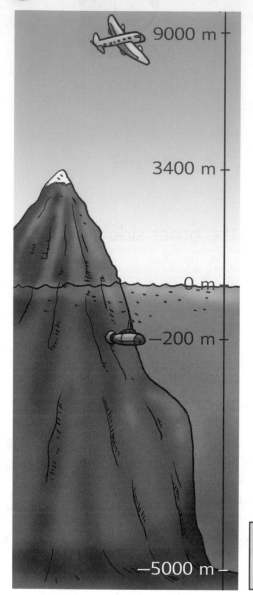

The height of a mountain or an airplane is measured by how far above sea level it is.

Sea level is 0 m.

The airplane is at 9000 m.

The mountain is 3400 m high.

The submarine is below sea level.

It is -200 m below sea level.

We use negative numbers for distances below sea level.

We use a negative sign '−' in the front of negative numbers.

The negative sign is also used as a symbol for subtraction.

The submarine is 200 m below sea level, or at negative two hundred meters.

The ocean floor is about -5000 m

below sea level, or negative ___ m.

1. Water freezes at 0 degrees Celsius. In the Antarctica, the temperature can be 3 degrees Celsius below freezing in January. We write this as −3 degrees Celsius. In July, the temperature can be 30 degrees below freezing. Write 30 degrees below freezing as a negative number.

2. Larry has no money. He has $0.
   Sally has ten dollars. She has $10.

   Paul owes ten dollars. He has -$10.

3. It is now ten minutes before a space shuttle will launch. The crew is checking the instruments.

   If launch is at 0 minutes, it is now

   -10 minutes.

now   launch
↓   ↓

—10 —9 —8 —7 —6 —5 —4 —3 —2 —1 0 +1 +2 +3 +4 +5 +6 +7 +8 +9 +10

Numbers to the right of 0 are called **positive numbers**. Examples are 1, 2, 3, 4. Numbers to the left of 0 are called **negative numbers**. Examples are −1, −2, −3, −4.

4. What number does each letter represent?

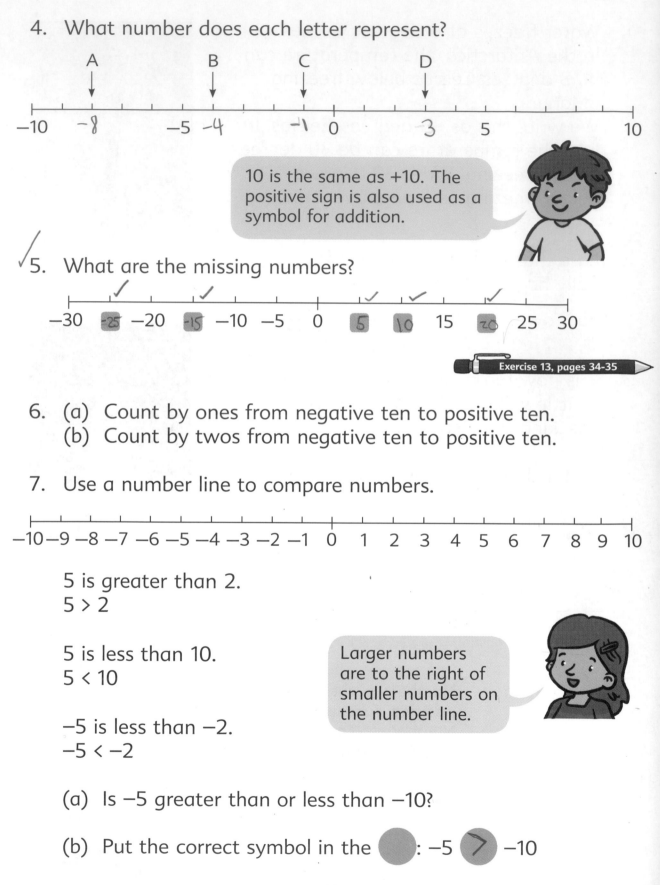

A   B   C   D
-8 -4 -1 3

10 is the same as +10. The positive sign is also used as a symbol for addition.

5. What are the missing numbers?

-30 -25 -20 -15 -10 -5 0 5 10 15 20 25 30

Exercise 13, pages 34-35

6. (a) Count by ones from negative ten to positive ten.
   (b) Count by twos from negative ten to positive ten.

7. Use a number line to compare numbers.

-10 -9 -8 -7 -6 -5 -4 -3 -2 -1 0 1 2 3 4 5 6 7 8 9 10

5 is greater than 2.
5 > 2

5 is less than 10.
5 < 10

-5 is less than -2.
-5 < -2

Larger numbers are to the right of smaller numbers on the number line.

(a) Is -5 greater than or less than -10?

(b) Put the correct symbol in the ⬤: -5 ⬤> -10

44

8. Write > or < in place of each 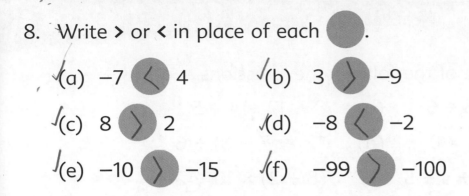.

(a) −7 < 4   (b) 3 > −9

(c) 8 > 2   (d) −8 < −2

(e) −10 > −15   (f) −99 > −100

9. Arrange the following numbers in increasing order.

   10, −8, 7, −5, 6

   −8 −5, 6, 7 10

10. (a) What number is 1 more than 5? 6

    (b) What number is 1 more than −5? -4

    (c) What number is 1 less than 0? − 1

    (d) What number is 2 less than −9? − 11

    (e) What number is 2 more than −2? 0

11. Complete the following regular number patterns.

    (a) 5, 4, 3, 2 , 1 , 0 , -1 , -2 , −3

    (b) 10, 8, 6, 4, 2, 0 , -2 , -4 , -6

45

Exercise 14, pages 36-37

1. Find the value of the following expressions.

   (a) $9 \times 7 - 6 \div 6$ (b) $8 - 12 \div 4 + 5$

   (c) $8 + 1 - 2 \times 0$ (d) $12 \times (7 - 6) \div 6$

   (e) $(12 - 8) \div 4 + 5$ (f) $(8 + 2) \times 10 \div 2$

   (g) $3 \times 7 + 3 \div 3$ (h) $1 + 2 \times (4 - 3)$

2. Find the number that goes into each ▢ to make the equations true.

   (a) $3 \times 4 + 6 = $ ▢ $+ 6$

   (b) $3 + 4 \div 2 = $ ▢ $+ 2$

   (c) $87 \times 4 = (80 + $ ▢ $) \times 4$

   (d) $6 \times (60 - $ ▢ $) = 6 \times 56$

   (e) $(4 \times 9) + (2 \times 1) = $ ▢ $+ 3$

   (f) $9 \times 123 = 9 \times (100 + $ ▢ $+ 3)$

3. Amy puts her photos into 2 albums. There are 24 pages in each album. She puts 6 photos on each page of the album. Which of the expressions below is **not** equal to the number of photos in the album?

   (a) $2 \times 24 \times 6$ (b) $24 \times 6 + 24 \times 6$

   (c) $24 + (2 \times 6)$ (d) $2 \times (20 + 4) \times 6$

4. What number does each letter represent?

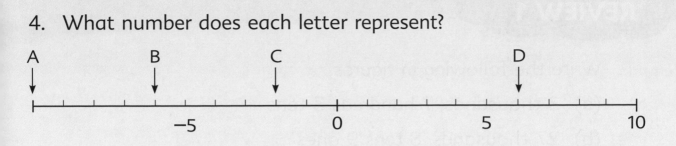

5. Arrange the following numbers in increasing order.

(a) 10, −9, 8, −7, 6

(b) −1, 1, 0, 2, −2

1. Write the following in figures.

    (a) 3 thousands, 7 hundreds 3 tens

    (b) 27 thousands, 8 tens 9 ones

    (c) 100 thousands

    (d) twelve hundred and four thousand, eight hundred three

    (e) seventy thousand million

    (f) negative forty-eight

2. Write the following in words.

    (a) 15,780   (b) 5,306,903   (c) −20,004

3. What is the value of the digit 6 in each of the following?

    (a) **6**54,020   (b) 1,234,**6**20   (c) **6**0,143

4. Complete the following number patterns.

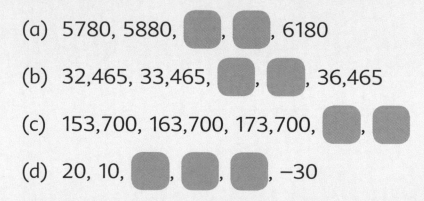

    (a) 5780, 5880, ⬜, ⬜, 6180

    (b) 32,465, 33,465, ⬜, ⬜, 36,465

    (c) 153,700, 163,700, 173,700, ⬜, ⬜

    (d) 20, 10, ⬜, ⬜, ⬜, −30

5. Write >, < or = in place of each ⬤ to make the number sentences true.

   (a) 3742 ⬤ 3714

   (b) 14,012,000 ⬤ 41,102,000

   (c) 56,375 ⬤ 6300 + 88

   (d) 700,000 ⬤ 7 × 100,000

6. Arrange the following numbers in increasing order.

   (a) 30,601,000, 30,061,000, 30,160,000, 30,016,000

   (b) 29,999, 90,000, 20,990, 29,909

   (c) 11, −2, 3, −8, 13, −21

   (d) 21, −18, 15, −12, 9, −6, 2

7. 6246 people attended a baseball game.
   Round the number of people to the nearest hundred.

8. Mount Everest is the highest mountain in the world.
   It is 29,028 ft high.
   Round this height to the nearest thousand ft.

9. Round the number 13,940,052 to

   (a) the nearest million.

   (b) the nearest hundred thousand.

   (c) the nearest ten thousand.

   (d) the nearest thousand.

10. (a) Is 3 a factor of 28?

    (b) Is 5 a factor of 60?

    (c) Is 6 a factor of 80?

    (d) Is 5 a factor of 92?

    (e) Is 4 a factor of 100?

11. What are the factors of 31?

12. Write a number in place of each 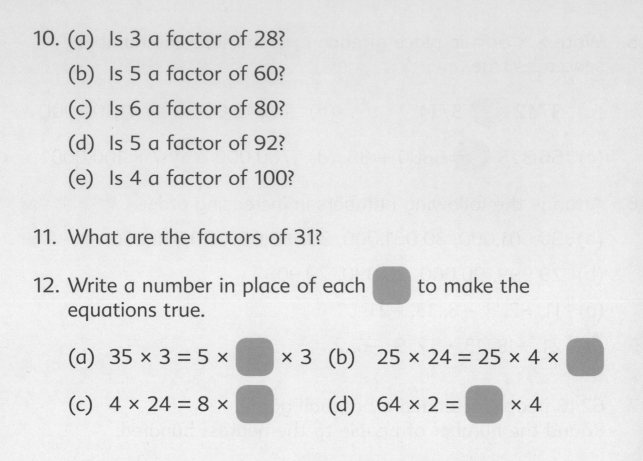 to make the equations true.

    (a) $35 \times 3 = 5 \times \boxed{} \times 3$ (b) $25 \times 24 = 25 \times 4 \times \boxed{}$

    (c) $4 \times 24 = 8 \times \boxed{}$ (d) $64 \times 2 = \boxed{} \times 4$

13. Find the value of each of the following expressions.

    (a) $4 + 32 \div 8$ (b) $6 \times (22 - 12)$

    (c) $40 - (3 \times 12) \div 6$ (d) $60 \div 10 - (4 + 2)$

14. What is the greatest whole number that can be placed in each 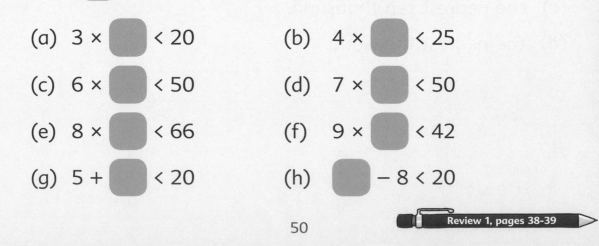 to make the number sentences true?

    (a) $3 \times \boxed{} < 20$ (b) $4 \times \boxed{} < 25$

    (c) $6 \times \boxed{} < 50$ (d) $7 \times \boxed{} < 50$

    (e) $8 \times \boxed{} < 66$ (f) $9 \times \boxed{} < 42$

    (g) $5 + \boxed{} < 20$ (h) $\boxed{} - 8 < 20$

Review 1, pages 38-39

2 THE FOUR OPERATIONS OF WHOLE NUMBERS

1 Addition and Subtraction

There are 3402 boys at a parade.
There are 987 more boys than girls.
(a) How many girls are there?

There are more boys than girls.

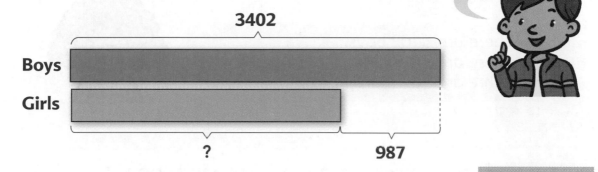

$$3402 - 987 = 2415$$

$$\begin{array}{r} {\scriptstyle 2\ \ 13\ \ 9\ \ 12} \\ 3\,4\,0\,2 \\ -\ \ \ \ 9\,8\,7 \\ \hline 2\,4\,1\,5 \end{array}$$

There are 2415 girls.

We can check the answer:
Does 2415 + 987 = 3402?

(b) How many children are there altogether?

$$3402 + 2415 = 5817$$

$$\begin{array}{r} 3\,4\,0\,2 \\ +\ \ 2\,4\,1\,5 \\ \hline 5\,8\,1\,7 \end{array}$$

There are 5817 children.

There are 3402 boys.
There are 2415 girls.
There are 5817 children altogether.

The **sum** of 3402 and 2415 is 5817.

There are 3402 boys.
There are 2415 girls.
There are 987 more boys than girls.

The **difference** between 3402 and 2415 is 987.

1. Find the sum of 864 and 659.

    864 + 659 =

    864   659

    ?

2. Find the difference between 674 and 467.

    674 − 467 =

    674

    467   ?

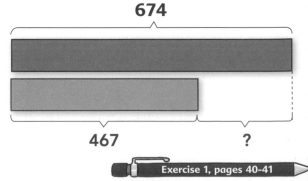

Exercise 1, pages 40–41

3. When 376 is subtracted from a number, the answer is 825.
   Find the number.

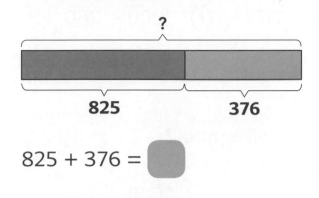

$\blacksquare - 376 = 825$

$825 + 376 = \boxed{}$

4. What number must be added to 462 to
   give the answer 1000?

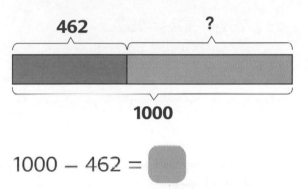

$462 + \blacksquare = 1000$

$1000 - 462 = \boxed{}$

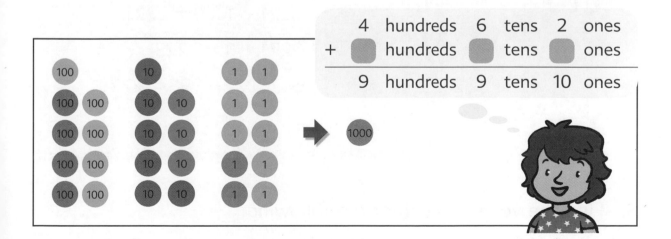

	4	hundreds	6	tens	2	ones
+	■	hundreds	■	tens	■	ones
	9	hundreds	9	tens	10	ones

5. Find the value of each of the following.

(a) $10 - 7 = 3$ (b) $100 - 7 = 93$ (c) $1000 - 7 = 993$
(d) $100 - 26 = 74$ (e) $1000 - 26 = 974$ (f) $1000 - 260 = 740$

Exercise 2, pages 42-43

6. Add 574 and 998.

Method 1:

$$\begin{array}{r} {\scriptstyle 1\ 1} \\ 5\,7\,4 \\ +\quad 9\,9\,8 \\ \hline 1\,5\,7\,2 \end{array}$$

Method 2:

$574 + 1000 = 1574$

$1574 - 2 = 1572$

So, $574 + 998 = 1572$

7. Subtract 998 from 3221.

Method 1:

$$\begin{array}{r} {\scriptstyle 2\ \ 11\ \ 11\ \ 11} \\ 3\,2\,2\,1 \\ -\quad 9\,9\,8 \\ \hline 2\,2\,2\,3 \end{array}$$

Method 2:

$3221 - 1000 = 2221$

$2221 + 2 = 2223$

So, $3221 - 998 = 2223$

8. Find the value of each of the following.

(a) $2436 + 9 = 2445$ (b) $2436 + 99 = 2535$ (c) $2436 + 999$
(d) $2436 - 9 =$ (e) $2436 - 99 =$ (f) $2436 - 999$

54

9. Add 2454 and 708.

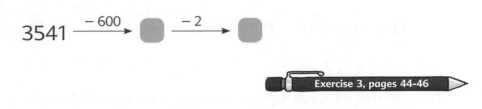

$$2454 \xrightarrow{+700} \square \xrightarrow{+8} \square$$

10. Subtract 602 from 3541.

$$3541 \xrightarrow{-600} \square \xrightarrow{-2} \square$$

Exercise 3, pages 44-46

11. Round each number to the nearest hundred.
    Then, estimate the value of 712 + 492.

$$712 \longrightarrow 700$$
$$492 \longrightarrow 500$$

$700 + 500 = \square$

The value of 712 + 492 is about $\square$.

12. Round each number to the nearest hundred.
    Then estimate the value of each of the following.

    (a) 384 + 296   (b) 507 + 892   (c) 914 + 707
    (d) 716 − 382   (e) 983 − 296   (f) 1408 − 693

13. Estimate the value of 786 − 297 + 518.

Round each number to the nearest hundred.
786 ⟶ 800
297 ⟶ 300
518 ⟶ 500

800 − 300 + 500 = ⬜

The value of 786 − 297 + 518 is about ⬜.

14. Estimate the value of each of the following.

(a) 418 + 293 + 108   (b) 784 + 617 + 399
(c) 814 + 208 − 587   (d) 1205 − 489 − 596

15. Jordan has $100. He wants to buy a watch that costs $39, a calculator that costs $14 and a book that costs $19. Does he have enough money?

I can use an estimate to see if I have enough money.

$40 + $10 + $20 = ⬜

He ⬜ enough money.

16. Lisa will win a prize if she sells 250 boxes of cookies. She sells 84 boxes in February and 62 boxes in March. How many more boxes does she have to sell to get the prize?

I want to find an exact number.

250 − 84 − 62 = ⬜

She has to sell ⬜ more boxes to get the prize.

Exercise 4, pages 47-48

17. There were 6020 spectators at a football game. 3860 of them were men, 2020 were women and the rest were children. How many children were there?

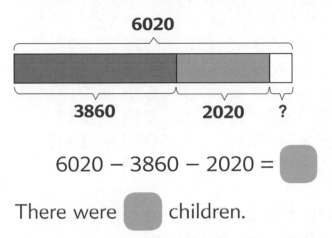

6020

3860   **2020**   **?**

6020 − 3860 − 2020 = ⬜

There were ⬜ children.

18. A farmer has 1025 ducks. He has 295 more chickens than ducks. How many chickens and ducks does he have altogether?

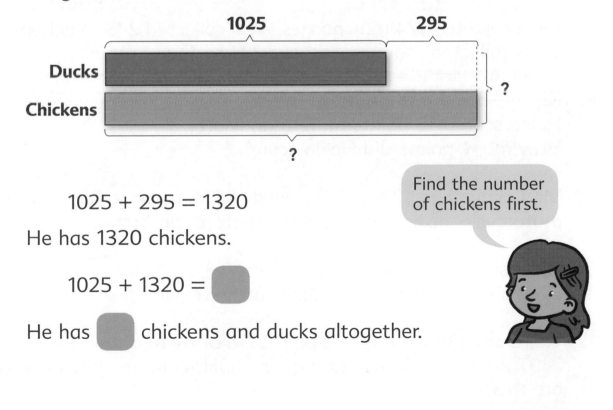

1025   **295**

Ducks

Chickens

?

?

Find the number of chickens first.

1025 + 295 = 1320

He has 1320 chickens.

1025 + 1320 = ⬜

He has ⬜ chickens and ducks altogether.

57

Exercise 5, pages 49-50

PRACTICE A

Find the value of each of the following.

	(a)	(b)	(c)
1.	431 + 99	652 + 999	576 + 998
2.	465 + 78	352 + 205	476 + 380
3.	476 − 99	206 − 98	628 − 199
4.	403 − 49	604 − 68	713 − 237
5.	2018 + 1447	1865 + 4154	5087 + 2993
6.	4661 − 2504	3050 − 2750	5000 − 1983

7. Round each number to the nearest hundred and then estimate the value of each of the following.

(a) 576 + 329   (b) 2154 + 887   (c) 3948 + 208
(d) 682 − 207   (e) 7078 − 238   (f) 5402 − 179
(g) 2590 + 109 − 484   (h) 1368 − 919 − 289

8. Ryan collected 174 matchboxes. Alan collected 243 matchboxes. Who collected more matchboxes? How many more?

9. Marty scored 438 points in a test.
Helen scored 15 points more than Marty.
How many points did Helen score?

10. Mr. Gomez has $2785. If he needs $536 more to buy a motorcycle, how much does the motorcycle cost?

11. Holly spent $99 and had $286 left.
How much money did she have at first?

12. There are 6345 beads in a bag. 3016 of them are white, 2107 are red, and the rest are green. How many green beads are there?

② Multiplication and Division

Sean has 1135 U.S. stamps. He has 3 times as many foreign stamps as U.S. stamps.

(a) How manys stamps does he have altogether?

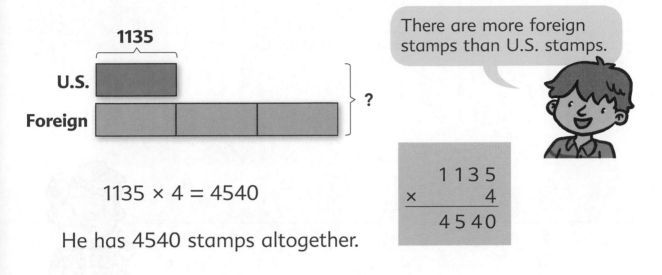

1135 × 4 = 4540

He has 4540 stamps altogether.

Multiply 1135 by 4.

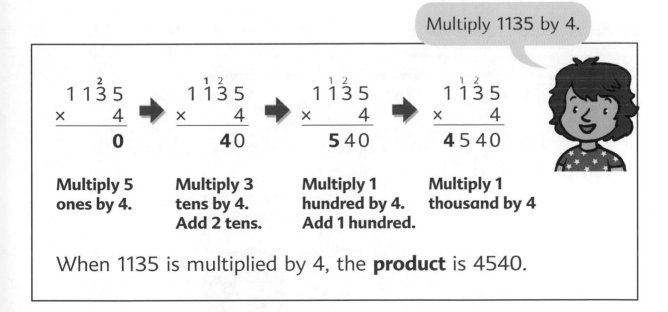

| Multiply 5 ones by 4. | Multiply 3 tens by 4. Add 2 tens. | Multiply 1 hundred by 4. Add 1 hundred. | Multiply 1 thousand by 4 |

When 1135 is multiplied by 4, the **product** is 4540.

(b) If Sean puts the stamps equally into 5 packets, how many stamps are there in each packet?

$$4540 \div 5 = 908$$

```
      9 0 8
5 ) 4 5 4 0
    4 5
      4 0
      4 0
          0
```

There are 908 stamps in each packet.

Divide 4540 by 5.

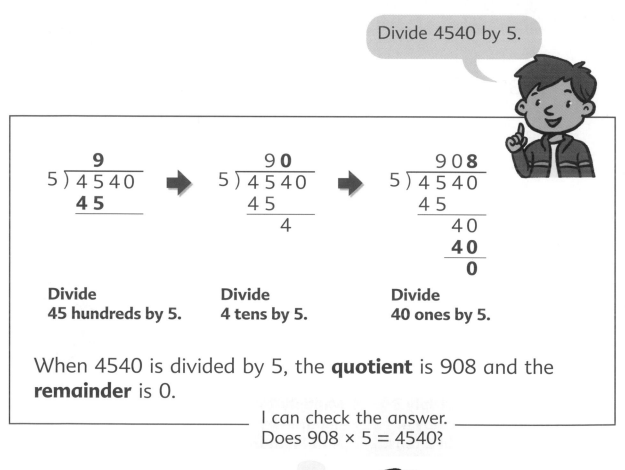

Divide
45 hundreds by 5.

Divide
4 tens by 5.

Divide
40 ones by 5.

When 4540 is divided by 5, the **quotient** is 908 and the **remainder** is 0.

I can check the answer.
Does 908 × 5 = 4540?

1. Multiply 3726 by 5.

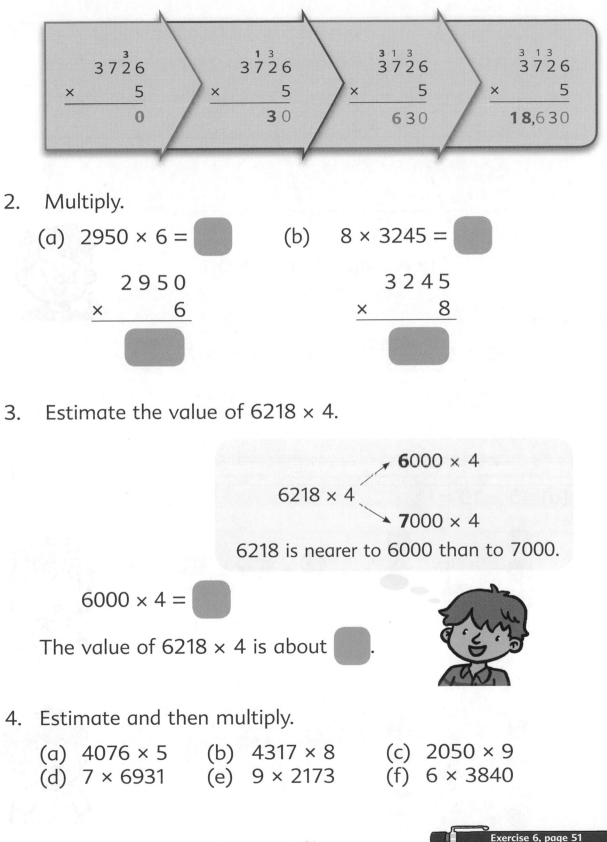

$$\begin{array}{r} \overset{3}{3}726 \\ \times \quad 5 \\ \hline 0 \end{array}$$

$$\begin{array}{r} \overset{1\ 3}{3}726 \\ \times \quad 5 \\ \hline 30 \end{array}$$

$$\begin{array}{r} \overset{3\ 1\ 3}{3}726 \\ \times \quad 5 \\ \hline 630 \end{array}$$

$$\begin{array}{r} \overset{3\ 1\ 3}{3}726 \\ \times \quad 5 \\ \hline 18,630 \end{array}$$

2. Multiply.

(a) 2950 × 6 = ▢

$$\begin{array}{r} 2950 \\ \times \quad 6 \\ \hline \end{array}$$

(b) 8 × 3245 = ▢

$$\begin{array}{r} 3245 \\ \times \quad 8 \\ \hline \end{array}$$

3. Estimate the value of 6218 × 4.

6218 × 4 ⟶ 6000 × 4
6218 × 4 ⟶ 7000 × 4

6218 is nearer to 6000 than to 7000.

6000 × 4 = ▢

The value of 6218 × 4 is about ▢.

4. Estimate and then multiply.

(a) 4076 × 5   (b) 4317 × 8   (c) 2050 × 9
(d) 7 × 6931   (e) 9 × 2173   (f) 6 × 3840

61

Exercise 6, page 51

5. Divide 4207 by 3.

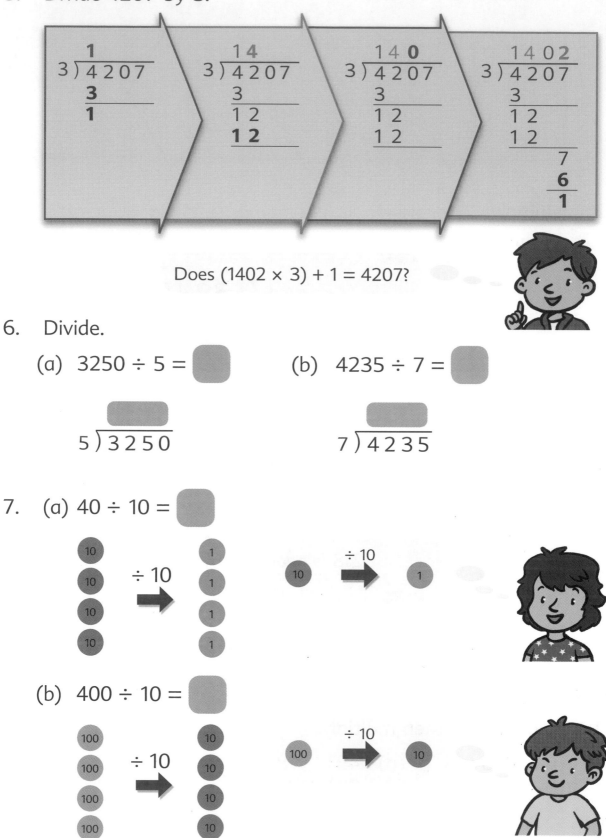

Does (1402 × 3) + 1 = 4207?

6. Divide.

(a) 3250 ÷ 5 = ☐

5)3250

(b) 4235 ÷ 7 = ☐

7)4235

7. (a) 40 ÷ 10 = ☐

(b) 400 ÷ 10 = ☐

(c) $440 \div 10 =$ ⬜

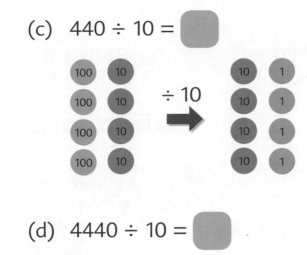

(d) $4440 \div 10 =$ ⬜

8. Estimate the value of $3840 \div 6$.

$3840 \div 6$ → $\textbf{36}00 \div 6$

$3840 \div 6$ → $\textbf{42}00 \div 6$

3840 is nearer to 3600 than to 4200.

$3600 \div 6 =$ ⬜

The value of $3840 \div 6$ is about ⬜.

9. Divide 3245 by 10.

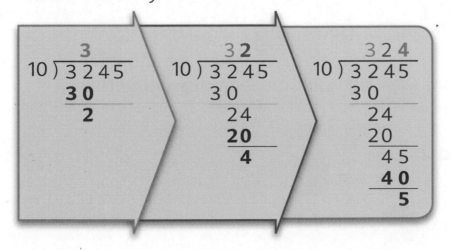

10. Estimate and then divide.

   (a) 3604 ÷ 9   (b) 3580 ÷ 7   (c) 3120 ÷ 8
   (d) 8128 ÷ 10   (e) 7528 ÷ 3   (f) 7180 ÷ 6

Exercise 7, pages 52-53

11. The number of cars is 4 times the number of motorcycles in a town.

   There are more cars than motorcycles.

   (a) If there are 4356 cars, how many motorcycles are there?

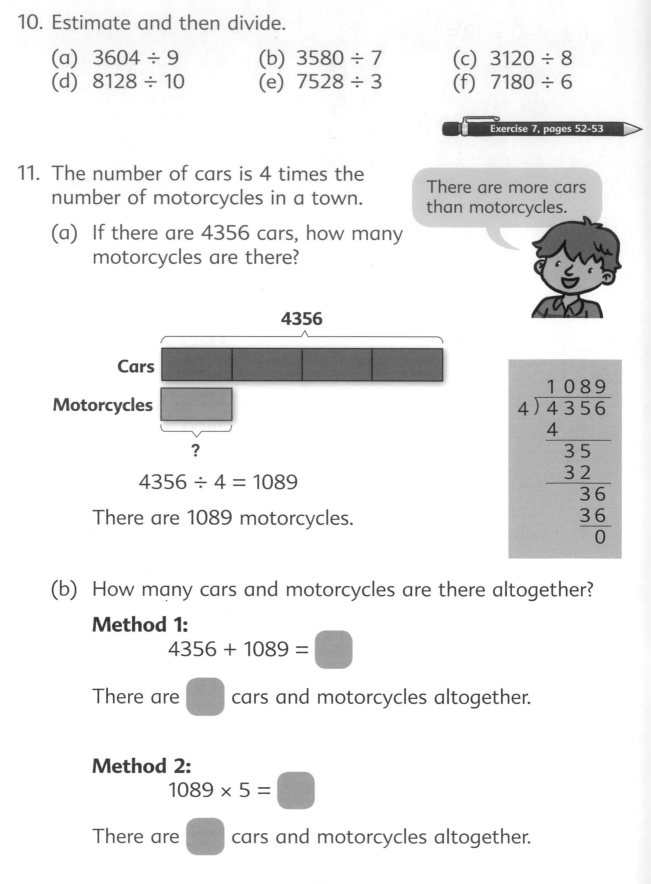

   4356 ÷ 4 = 1089

   There are 1089 motorcycles.

   (b) How many cars and motorcycles are there altogether?

   Method 1:

   4356 + 1089 = ⬜

   There are ⬜ cars and motorcycles altogether.

   Method 2:

   1089 × 5 = ⬜

   There are ⬜ cars and motorcycles altogether.

64

12. Mr. Cohen earns $2935 a month. If he spends $1780 each month and saves the rest, how much will he save in 6 months?

2935 − 1780 = 1155

He saves $1155 each month.

1155 × 6 =

He will save $⬚ in 6 months.

First, I find the amount Mr. Cohen saves each month.

13. David bought 6 cameras at $1340 each. Then he bought another 8 cameras at $1248 each. How much did he spend altogether?

1340 × 6 = 8040

He spent $8040 on the first 6 cameras.

1248 × 8 = 9984

He spent $9984 on the next 8 cameras.

8040 + 9984 = ⬚

He spent $⬚ altogether.

First, I find the total amount David spent on the first 6 cameras. Then, I find the total amount he spent on the next 8 cameras.

14. A school wants to know how many loaves of bread it needs to order for 390 students such that each student will have 3 meals with 1 serving of bread. About 5 servings can be made from 1 loaf of bread. About how many loaves of bread should be ordered?

The school just needs an estimated number of servings. So, round 390 to the nearest hundred.

Number of servings = 400 × 3
= 1200

We need a more exact answer at this step so we will not order too many loaves!

Number of loaves of bread = 1200 ÷ 5
=

About ___ loaves of bread should be ordered.

Exercise 8, pages 54-55

Estimate and then find the value of each of the following expressions.

	(a)	(b)	(c)
1.	2011 × 3	2107 × 4	3450 × 5
2.	4215 × 6	3917 × 7	6258 × 9
3.	2109 ÷ 3	4036 ÷ 4	2510 ÷ 5
4.	7212 ÷ 6	3968 ÷ 8	8181 ÷ 9
5.	6431 ÷ 7	4750 ÷ 10	3299 ÷ 10

6. A baker sold 1380 cakes last month.
   He sold 3 times as many cakes this month as last month.
   How many cakes did he sell this month?

7. The cost of a computer is 4 times the cost of a printer.
   If the computer costs $2560, find the cost of the printer.

8. Josh had 1536 rubber bands.
   He put them equally into 6 boxes.
   How many rubber bands were there in each box?

9. James bought 3750 kg of potatoes. He
   packed the potatoes into bags of 10 kg each.
   How many bags of potatoes did he have?

10. The total cost of a scooter and 2 motorcycles is $9798.
    The cost of each motorcycle is $3654.
    Find the cost of the scooter.

11. For the last four months, Jake earned a fixed sum of money
    monthly. During this period, he spent $3032 and saved the
    remaining $4548. How much did Jake earn each month?

❸ Multiplication by a 2-Digit Number

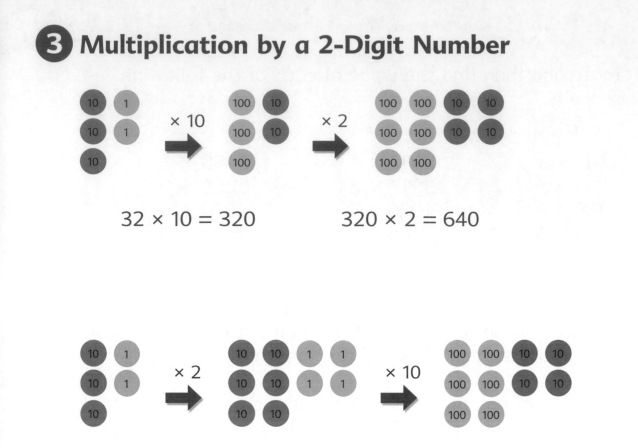

32 × 10 = 320   320 × 2 = 640

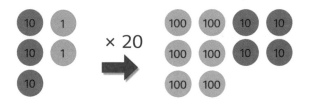

32 × 2 = 64   64 × 10 = 640

32 × 20 = 640

1. Multiply.

   (a) 16 × 10   (b) 40 × 10   (c) 254 × 10
   (d) 10 × 29   (e) 10 × 96   (f) 10 × 380

2. Find the product of 14 and 30.

   Method 1:
   14 × 30 = 14 × 10 × 3
            = 140 × 3
            =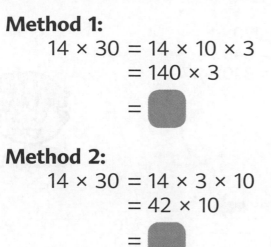

   Method 2:
   14 × 30 = 14 × 3 × 10
            = 42 × 10
            =

   Method 3:
   14 × 3 = 42
   14 × 3**0** = 42**0**

3. Multiply.

   (a) 284 × 20 =    (b) 40 × 309 =

   ```
         2 8 4                        3 0 9
   ×        2 0                 ×        4 0
       5 6 8 0                   12,3 6 0
   ```

69

4. Multiply.

    (a) 23 × 30   (b) 68 × 70   (c) 392 × 80

    (d) 50 × 36   (e) 90 × 45   (f) 560 × 60

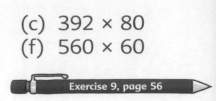 Exercise 9, page 56

5. Multiply 34 by 15.

$34 \times 15 = \boxed{}$

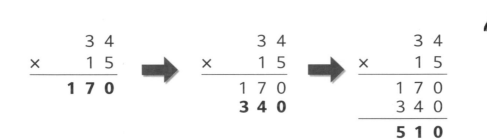

34 × 5 = 170
34 × 10 = 340
34 × 15 = 340 + 170

```
      3 4              3 4              3 4
  ×   1 5          ×   1 5          ×   1 5
  ───────          ───────          ───────
    1 7 0            1 7 0            1 7 0
                     3 4 0            3 4 0
                                    ───────
                                      5 1 0
```

6. Multiply.

    (a) 64 × 27 = $\boxed{}$

```
        6 4
    ×   2 7
    ─────────
      4 4 8   ←──── 64 × 7
    1 2 8 0   ←──── 64 × 20
    ─────────
    1 7 2 8
```

(b) $19 \times 278 = \boxed{}$

Method 1:

$$
\begin{array}{r}
2\ 7\ 8 \\
\times\ \ \ \ 1\ 9 \\
\hline
2\ 5\ 0\ 2 \\
2\ 7\ 8\ 0 \\
\hline
5\ 2\ 8\ 2
\end{array}
$$

$2502 \longleftarrow 278 \times 9$
$2780 \longleftarrow 278 \times 10$

Method 2:

$19 \times 278 = 20 \times 278 - 278$

$20 \times 278 = 5560$
$19 \times 278 = 5560 - 278 = 5282$

(c) $36 \times 99 = \boxed{}$

$36 \times 99 = 36 \times 100 - 36$

$36 \times 100 = 3600$
$36 \times 99\ \ = 3600 - 36$
$ = \boxed{}$

(d) $28 \times 25 = \boxed{}$

$4 \times 25 = 100$

$\mathbf{28} \times 25 = \mathbf{7} \times \mathbf{4} \times 25$
$ = 7 \times 100$
$ = \boxed{}$

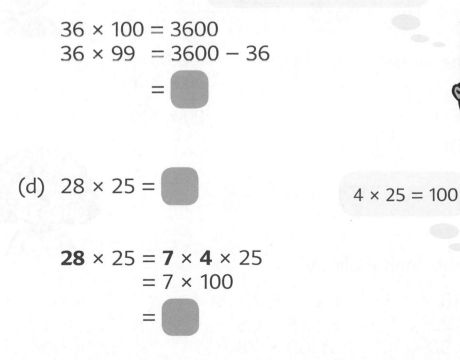

7. Multiply.

(a) 8 × 99   (b) 24 × 99   (c) 36 × 99
(d) 99 × 9   (e) 99 × 47   (f) 99 × 38

8. Multiply.

(a) 8 × 25   (b) 36 × 25   (c) 44 × 25
(d) 25 × 12   (e) 25 × 52   (f) 25 × 72

Exercise 10, page 57

9. Multiply.

(a) 20 × 60   (b) 50 × 80   (c) 70 × 90
(d) 500 × 30   (e) 40 × 600   (f) 400 × 50

10. Estimate the value of 32 × 68.

$$32 × 68$$
$$↓ \quad ↓$$
$$30 × 70$$

30 × 70 = ⬜

The value of 32 × 68 is about ⬜.

11. Estimate the value of 48 × 315.

$$48 × 315$$
$$↓ \quad ↓$$
$$50 × 300$$

50 × 300 = ⬜

The value of 48 × 315 is about ⬜.

12. Estimate and then multiply.

(a) 49 × 18   (b) 21 × 72   (c) 62 × 47
(d) 412 × 23   (e) 383 × 58   (f) 685 × 32
(g) 51 × 490   (h) 69 × 786   (i) 88 × 594

Exercise 11, pages 58-60

Estimate and then find the value of each of the following.

	(a)	(b)	(c)
1.	2907 × 4	6032 × 5	7902 × 7
2.	4170 ÷ 6	5616 ÷ 8	8019 ÷ 9
3.	48 × 11	61 × 29	88 × 67
4.	101 ×13	289 × 53	786 × 78

5. Miguel delivers 165 copies of a newspaper every day. How many copies of the newspaper will he deliver in 30 days?

6. Tom bought 15 sheets of stamps. If there were 25 stamps on each sheet, how many stamps did he buy?

7. After buying 12 chairs at $128 each, Catherine had $342 left. How much money did she have at first?

8. 300 children are divided into two groups. There are 50 more children in the first group than in the second group. How many children are there in the second group?

9. The difference between two numbers is 2184. If the bigger number is 3 times the smaller number, find the sum of the two numbers.

10. Mrs. Garcia saved $2001 in two years. She saved $65 a month in the first 15 months. She saved the same amount every month in the next 9 months. How much did she save a month in the next 9 months?

Exercise 12, pages 61-62

1. What is the value of the digit **6** in each of the following?
    (a) 39,1**6**4   (b) **16**,083   (c) **6**23,750

2. Write the following in figures.
    (a) twenty-four thousand, thirty-eight
    (b) seventy-four thousand, two
    (c) four million, three hundred thousand, seven hundred eight
    (d) negative one hundred

3. Write the following in words.
    (a) 42,310   (b) 15,206   (c) 208,150

4. Bill has $2486 in his savings account. Round this amount of money to the nearest hundred dollars.

5. (a) Write down a common factor of 12 and 20.
    (b) Write down a common multiple of 8 and 12.

6. Find the sum of each of the following.
    (a) 980 and 2520   (b) 7998 and 2002
    (c) 263, 3478 and 8723   (d) 999, 1001 and 8000

7. Find the difference between each of the following.
    (a) 2516 and 78   (b) 5021 and 996
    (c) 7605 and 6996   (d) 6702 and 8000

8. Find the product of each of the following.
    (a) 85 and 6   (b) 928 and 7
    (c) 64 and 25   (d) 1250 and 8

9. Find the quotient and remainder when
   (a) 1026 is divided by 3.   (b) 5000 is divided by 6.
   (c) 4984 is divided by 7.   (d) 2831 is divided by 9.

10. Write **>**, **<**, or **=** in the 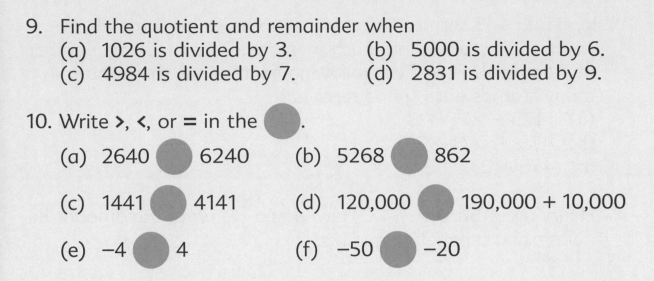.

   (a) 2640 ⬤ 6240   (b) 5268 ⬤ 862

   (c) 1441 ⬤ 4141   (d) 120,000 ⬤ 190,000 + 10,000

   (e) −4 ⬤ 4   (f) −50 ⬤ −20

11. What is the number represented by k in each of the following?
   (a) 260 tens = k
   (b) 1,000,000 + 600,00 + k = 1,620,000
   (c) 27,400 = k + 400   (d) 400 = k × 400

12. What is the greatest whole number that can be

   placed in each 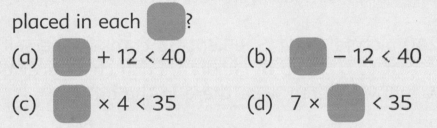?

   (a) ⬛ + 12 < 40   (b) ⬛ − 12 < 40

   (c) ⬛ × 4 < 35   (d) 7 × ⬛ < 35

13. (a) What number is 10,000 less than 100,000?
    (b) What number is 1000 less than 100,000?
    (c) What number is 100 less than 100,000?
    (d) What number is 10 less than 100,000?
    (e) What number is 1 less than 100,000?

14. What is the number represented by n to make each of the
    following equations true?
    (a) 4 × 8 × 3 = n × 3 × 4   (b) 3 + 2 + 9 = 18 − n
    (c) 409 − 79 = 409 − 80 + n (d) 18 × 12 = 180 + n
    (e) 42 × 99 = 4200 − n (f) 12 × 25 = 3 × n
    (g) 72 ÷ (15 − 6) = n ÷ 9   (h) (3 + 4) × (12 − 6) = 7 × n
    (i) 100 ÷ 1 = (33 × 3) + n (j) 400 − 32 = 300 + n

75

15. John had 475 stamps. After giving some to his 3 friends, he had 271 stamps left. Each friend received the same number of stamps. Which of the following expressions shows how many stamps each friend received?
    (a) $(475 - 271) \div 3$
    (b) $475 - (271 \div 3)$
    (c) $475 - 271 \div 3$

16. Henry owes Barbara $48. How would we write the amount he owes using a negative number?

17. Arrange these numbers in order from the smallest:
    4, −2, 3, −4, 11, −12

18. A shopkeeper packed 3284 cakes of soap into 6 equal packages.
    (a) How many cakes of soap were there in each package?
    (b) How many cakes of soap were left over?

19. Mary had 1240 picture cards. She kept 80 cards for herself and gave the rest to a group of children. Each child received 8 cards. How many children were there in the group?

20. 3000 exercise books are arranged in 3 piles. The first pile has 10 more books than the second pile. The number of books in the second pile is twice the number of books in the third pile. How many books are there in the third pile?

Review 2, pages 63-66

3 FRACTIONS

1 Equivalent Fractions

Mandy, Serena and Alex each bought a pizza of the same size.

I cut the pizza into 3 equal parts and ate 1 part.
I ate $\frac{1}{3}$ of the pizza.

I cut the pizza into 6 equal parts and ate 2 parts. I ate $\frac{2}{6}$ of the pizza.

I cut the pizza into 9 equal parts and ate 3 parts. I ate $\frac{3}{9}$ of the pizza.

$$\frac{1}{3} = \frac{2}{6} = \frac{3}{9}$$

$\frac{1}{3}$, $\frac{2}{6}$ and $\frac{3}{9}$ are **equivalent fractions**.

$\frac{1}{3}$ **is a fraction in its simplest form.**

1. What are the missing numerators and denominators?

(a)

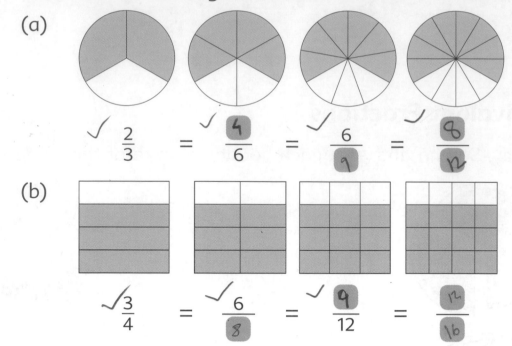

✓ $\dfrac{2}{3}$ = ✓ $\dfrac{4}{6}$ = ✓ $\dfrac{6}{9}$ = ✓ $\dfrac{8}{12}$

(b)

✓ $\dfrac{3}{4}$ = ✓ $\dfrac{6}{8}$ = ✓ $\dfrac{9}{12}$ = $\dfrac{12}{16}$

Find the missing numerator or denominator.

✓

2. (a) ✓ $\dfrac{4}{5} \overset{\times 2}{\underset{\times 2}{=}} \dfrac{8}{10}$

(b) ✓ $\dfrac{1}{4} \overset{\times 3}{\underset{\times 3}{=}} \dfrac{3}{12}$

(c) ✓ $\dfrac{1}{6} = \dfrac{4}{24}$

(d) ✓ $\dfrac{2}{3} = \dfrac{10}{15}$

3. (a) ✓ $\dfrac{8}{12} \overset{\div 2}{\underset{\div 2}{=}} \dfrac{4}{6}$

(b) ✓ $\dfrac{9}{15} \overset{\div 3}{\underset{\div 3}{=}} \dfrac{3}{5}$

(c) ✓ $\dfrac{12}{16} = \dfrac{3}{4}$

(d) ✓ $\dfrac{5}{20} = \dfrac{1}{4}$

4. Express each of the following fractions in its simplest form.

(a) $\dfrac{9}{18}$ $\dfrac{1}{2}$ (b) $\dfrac{12}{18}$ $\dfrac{2}{3}$ (c) $\dfrac{10}{12}$ $\dfrac{5}{6}$ (d) $\dfrac{16}{20}$ $\dfrac{4}{5}$

Exercise 1, pages 67-68

5. Arrange the fractions in increasing order,

(a) $\frac{3}{5}$, $\frac{1}{2}$, $\frac{9}{10}$

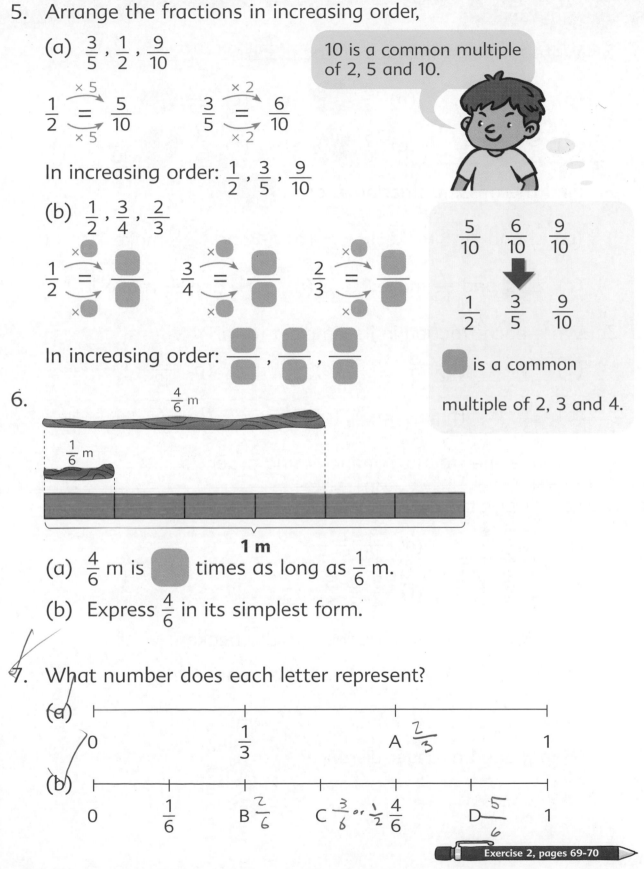

10 is a common multiple of 2, 5 and 10.

$\frac{1}{2} \xrightarrow[\times 5]{\times 5} \frac{5}{10}$ $\frac{3}{5} \xrightarrow[\times 2]{\times 2} \frac{6}{10}$

In increasing order: $\frac{1}{2}$, $\frac{3}{5}$, $\frac{9}{10}$

(b) $\frac{1}{2}$, $\frac{3}{4}$, $\frac{2}{3}$

$\frac{1}{2} = \frac{}{}$ $\frac{3}{4} = \frac{}{}$ $\frac{2}{3} = \frac{}{}$

In increasing order: $\frac{}{}$, $\frac{}{}$, $\frac{}{}$

$\frac{5}{10}$ $\frac{6}{10}$ $\frac{9}{10}$

$\frac{1}{2}$ $\frac{3}{5}$ $\frac{9}{10}$

is a common multiple of 2, 3 and 4.

6.

$\frac{4}{6}$ m

$\frac{1}{6}$ m

1 m

(a) $\frac{4}{6}$ m is ⬛ times as long as $\frac{1}{6}$ m.

(b) Express $\frac{4}{6}$ in its simplest form.

7. What number does each letter represent?

(a)
0        $\frac{1}{3}$ A $\frac{2}{3}$ 1

(b)
0    $\frac{1}{6}$ B $\frac{2}{6}$ C $\frac{3}{6}$ or $\frac{1}{2}$ $\frac{4}{6}$ D $\frac{5}{6}$ 1

Exercise 2, pages 69-70

1. Write **>**, **<**, or **=** in place of each 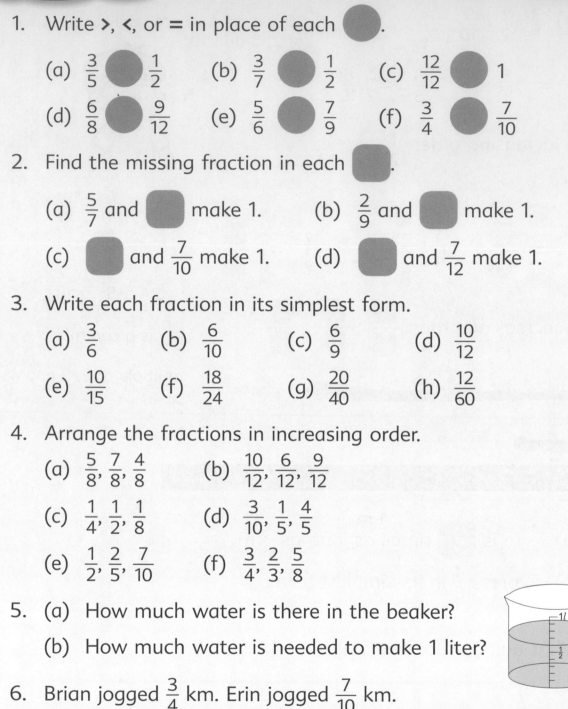.

   (a) $\frac{3}{5}$ ⬤ $\frac{1}{2}$ (b) $\frac{3}{7}$ ⬤ $\frac{1}{2}$ (c) $\frac{12}{12}$ ⬤ 1

   (d) $\frac{6}{8}$ ⬤ $\frac{9}{12}$ (e) $\frac{5}{6}$ ⬤ $\frac{7}{9}$ (f) $\frac{3}{4}$ ⬤ $\frac{7}{10}$

2. Find the missing fraction in each ⬛.

   (a) $\frac{5}{7}$ and ⬛ make 1.   (b) $\frac{2}{9}$ and ⬛ make 1.

   (c) ⬛ and $\frac{7}{10}$ make 1.   (d) ⬛ and $\frac{7}{12}$ make 1.

3. Write each fraction in its simplest form.

   (a) $\frac{3}{6}$ (b) $\frac{6}{10}$ (c) $\frac{6}{9}$ (d) $\frac{10}{12}$

   (e) $\frac{10}{15}$ (f) $\frac{18}{24}$ (g) $\frac{20}{40}$ (h) $\frac{12}{60}$

4. Arrange the fractions in increasing order.

   (a) $\frac{5}{8}, \frac{7}{8}, \frac{4}{8}$ (b) $\frac{10}{12}, \frac{6}{12}, \frac{9}{12}$

   (c) $\frac{1}{4}, \frac{1}{2}, \frac{1}{8}$ (d) $\frac{3}{10}, \frac{1}{5}, \frac{4}{5}$

   (e) $\frac{1}{2}, \frac{2}{5}, \frac{7}{10}$ (f) $\frac{3}{4}, \frac{2}{3}, \frac{5}{8}$

5. (a) How much water is there in the beaker?

   (b) How much water is needed to make 1 liter?

6. Brian jogged $\frac{3}{4}$ km. Erin jogged $\frac{7}{10}$ km.

   Who jogged a longer distance?

② Adding and Subtracting Fractions

Chrissy, Sharon and Paul shared a pizza.

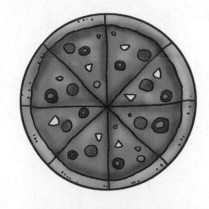

Chrissy ate $\frac{3}{8}$ of the pizza.

Sharon ate $\frac{1}{8}$ of the pizza.

Paul ate $\frac{1}{4}$ of the pizza.

What fraction of the pizza did Chrissy and Sharon eat?

The pizza is divided into 8 equal parts. Chrissy ate 3 parts and Sharon ate 1 part.
3 eighths + 1 eighth = 4 eighths

Add $\frac{3}{8}$ and $\frac{1}{8}$.

$$\frac{3}{8} + \frac{1}{8} = \frac{4}{8}$$

$$= \boxed{}$$

Always write your answer in the simplest form.
4 eighths = 1 half

Chrissy and Sharon ate $\boxed{}$ of the pizza.

What fraction of the pizza did they eat altogether?

$$\frac{3}{8} + \frac{1}{8} + \frac{1}{4} = \frac{3}{8} + \frac{1}{8} + \frac{2}{8}$$

$$= \boxed{}$$

$$= \boxed{}$$

One fourth of the pizza is the same as two eighths. Paul ate two eighths of the pizza.

We can also add $\frac{1}{2}$ and $\frac{1}{4}$.

$$\frac{1}{2} + \frac{1}{4} = \frac{\boxed{}}{4} + \frac{1}{4}$$

$$= \boxed{}$$

Before we add or subtract fractions, we change them to fractions with the same denominator.

Altogether, the three children

ate of the pizza.

How much pizza was left?

$$1 - \frac{3}{4} = \frac{4}{4} - \frac{3}{4} = \frac{1}{4}$$

$$1 = \frac{4}{4}$$

1. Add or subtract.

    (a) $\frac{1}{7} + \frac{4}{7}$ (b) $\frac{1}{6} + \frac{3}{6}$ (c) $\frac{5}{12} + \frac{1}{12}$

    (b) $\frac{7}{9} - \frac{3}{9}$ (e) $\frac{7}{10} - \frac{3}{10}$ (f) $1 - \frac{5}{8}$

    (g) $\frac{1}{5} + \frac{2}{5} + \frac{2}{5}$ (h) $1 - \frac{3}{4} - \frac{1}{4}$ (i) $1 - \frac{5}{9} + \frac{2}{9}$

2. Add $\frac{2}{3}$ and $\frac{1}{6}$.

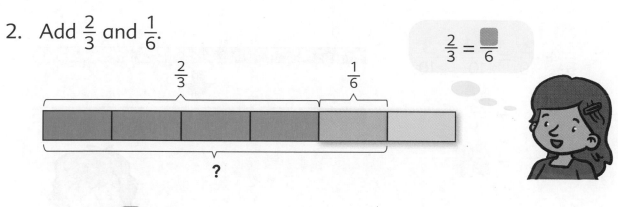

$\frac{2}{3} = \frac{\boxed{}}{6}$

$\frac{2}{3} + \frac{1}{6} = \frac{\boxed{}}{6} + \frac{1}{6}$

$\phantom{\frac{2}{3} + \frac{1}{6}} = \frac{\boxed{}}{6}$

3. What are the missing numbers?

    (a) $\frac{3}{8} + \frac{1}{4}$ (b) $\frac{2}{3} + \frac{1}{9}$

    $= \frac{3}{8} + \frac{\boxed{}}{8}$ $= \frac{\boxed{}}{9} + \frac{1}{9}$

    $= \frac{\boxed{}}{8}$ $= \frac{\boxed{}}{9}$

4. Add $\frac{1}{5}$ and $\frac{3}{10}$.

$$\frac{1}{5} = \frac{\boxed{}}{10}$$

$$\frac{1}{5} + \frac{3}{10} = \frac{\boxed{}}{10} + \frac{3}{10}$$

$$= \frac{\boxed{}}{10}$$

$$= \boxed{}$$

5. What are the missing numbers?

(a) $\frac{1}{3} + \frac{1}{6}$

$$= \frac{\boxed{}}{6} + \frac{1}{6}$$

$$= \frac{\boxed{}}{6}$$

$$= \boxed{}$$

(b) $\frac{1}{2} + \frac{3}{10}$

$$= \frac{\boxed{}}{10} + \frac{3}{10}$$

$$= \frac{\boxed{}}{10}$$

$$= \boxed{}$$

6. Add.

(a) $\frac{1}{2} + \frac{1}{8}$

(b) $\frac{1}{4} + \frac{2}{12}$

(c) $\frac{2}{3} + \frac{1}{9}$

(d) $\frac{1}{2} + \frac{1}{6}$

(e) $\frac{2}{5} + \frac{1}{10}$

(f) $\frac{2}{3} + \frac{1}{12}$

(g) $\frac{1}{5} + \frac{3}{10}$

(h) $\frac{1}{6} + \frac{7}{12}$

(i) $\frac{3}{4} + \frac{1}{12}$

(j) $\frac{1}{3} + \frac{1}{9} + \frac{1}{9}$

(k) $\frac{1}{2} + \frac{1}{4} + \frac{1}{4}$

(l) $\frac{1}{4} + \frac{1}{8} + \frac{3}{8}$

84

Exercise 3, pages 71-72

7. Subtract $\frac{1}{8}$ from $\frac{1}{2}$.

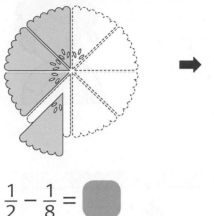

1 half = 4 eighths

$\frac{1}{2} - \frac{1}{8} = \boxed{}$

8. Subtract $\frac{1}{2}$ from $\frac{7}{8}$.

$\frac{1}{2} = \frac{\boxed{}}{8}$

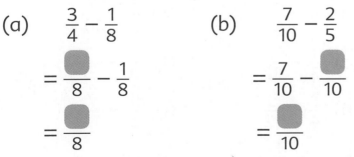

$\frac{7}{8} - \frac{1}{2} = \frac{7}{8} - \frac{\boxed{}}{8}$

$\qquad = \frac{\boxed{}}{8}$

9. What are the missing numbers?

(a) $\frac{3}{4} - \frac{1}{8}$

$\quad = \frac{\boxed{}}{8} - \frac{1}{8}$

$\quad = \frac{\boxed{}}{8}$

(b) $\frac{7}{10} - \frac{2}{5}$

$\quad = \frac{7}{10} - \frac{\boxed{}}{10}$

$\quad = \frac{\boxed{}}{10}$

10. Subtract $\frac{5}{12}$ from $\frac{3}{4}$.

$$\frac{3}{4} = \frac{\square}{12}$$

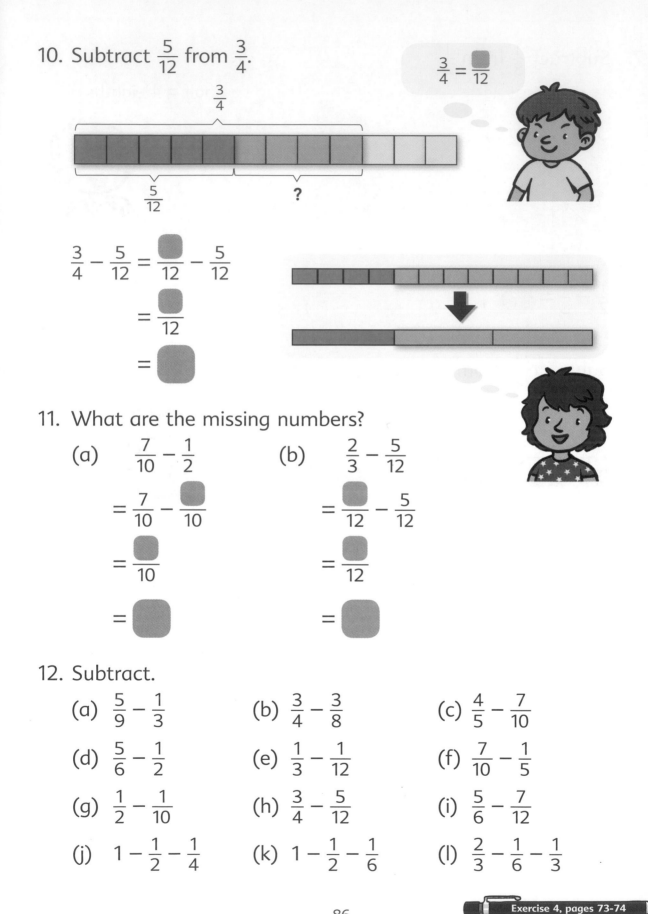

$$\frac{3}{4} - \frac{5}{12} = \frac{\square}{12} - \frac{5}{12}$$

$$= \frac{\square}{12}$$

$$= \square$$

11. What are the missing numbers?

(a) $\frac{7}{10} - \frac{1}{2}$

$= \frac{7}{10} - \frac{\square}{10}$

$= \frac{\square}{10}$

$= \square$

(b) $\frac{2}{3} - \frac{5}{12}$

$= \frac{\square}{12} - \frac{5}{12}$

$= \frac{\square}{12}$

$= \square$

12. Subtract.

(a) $\frac{5}{9} - \frac{1}{3}$

(b) $\frac{3}{4} - \frac{3}{8}$

(c) $\frac{4}{5} - \frac{7}{10}$

(d) $\frac{5}{6} - \frac{1}{2}$

(e) $\frac{1}{3} - \frac{1}{12}$

(f) $\frac{7}{10} - \frac{1}{5}$

(g) $\frac{1}{2} - \frac{1}{10}$

(h) $\frac{3}{4} - \frac{5}{12}$

(i) $\frac{5}{6} - \frac{7}{12}$

(j) $1 - \frac{1}{2} - \frac{1}{4}$

(k) $1 - \frac{1}{2} - \frac{1}{6}$

(l) $\frac{2}{3} - \frac{1}{6} - \frac{1}{3}$

86

Exercise 4, pages 73-74

Add or subtract.

	(a)	(b)	(c)
1.	$\dfrac{7}{8} - \dfrac{3}{4}$	$\dfrac{2}{3} - \dfrac{1}{12}$	$1 - \dfrac{3}{10}$
2.	$\dfrac{2}{9} + \dfrac{1}{3}$	$\dfrac{1}{6} + \dfrac{2}{3}$	$\dfrac{5}{12} + \dfrac{1}{4}$
3.	$\dfrac{1}{6} - \dfrac{1}{12}$	$\dfrac{3}{8} - \dfrac{1}{4}$	$\dfrac{4}{5} - \dfrac{3}{10}$
4.	$\dfrac{1}{2} + \dfrac{3}{8}$	$\dfrac{1}{3} + \dfrac{1}{12}$	$\dfrac{2}{8} + \dfrac{3}{4}$
5.	$\dfrac{1}{4} + \dfrac{3}{8} + \dfrac{1}{4}$	$\dfrac{7}{8} - \dfrac{1}{8} - \dfrac{3}{8}$	$1 - \dfrac{1}{5} - \dfrac{3}{10}$

6. Mary has $\dfrac{3}{4}$ liter of orange juice.

   She drinks $\dfrac{1}{2}$ liter of it.

   How much orange juice does she have left?

7. Mr. Johnson bought a can of paint.

   He used $\dfrac{1}{2}$ of it to paint a table.

   He used $\dfrac{1}{8}$ of it to paint a book shelf.

   How much paint did he use altogether?

8. Meredith bought $\dfrac{2}{5}$ kg of sugar. Courtney bought $\dfrac{1}{10}$ kg of sugar less than Meredith.

   (a) Find the weight of sugar bought by Courtney.
   (b) Find the total weight of sugar bought by both of them.

Exercise 5, pages 75-76

③ Mixed Numbers

This strip of paper is longer than 1 m.

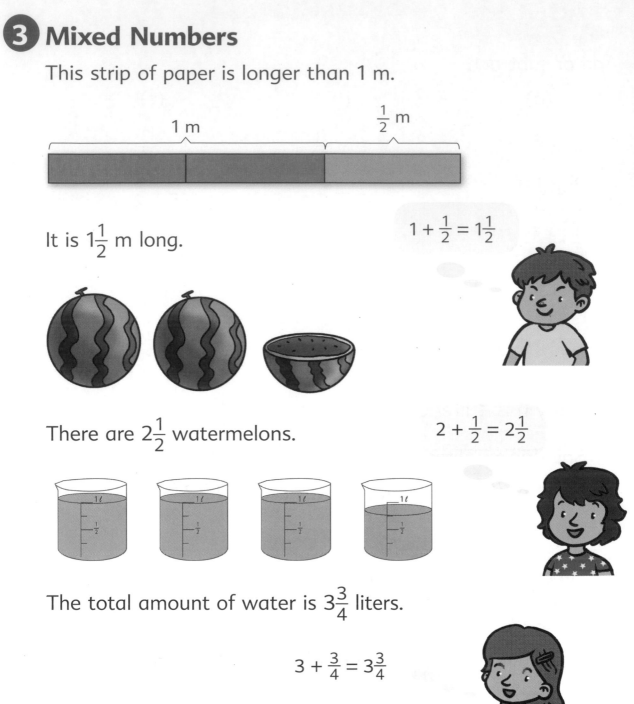

1 m

$\frac{1}{2}$ m

It is $1\frac{1}{2}$ m long.

$1 + \frac{1}{2} = 1\frac{1}{2}$

There are $2\frac{1}{2}$ watermelons.

$2 + \frac{1}{2} = 2\frac{1}{2}$

The total amount of water is $3\frac{3}{4}$ liters.

$$3 + \frac{3}{4} = 3\frac{3}{4}$$

$1\frac{1}{2}$, $2\frac{1}{2}$ and $3\frac{3}{4}$ are **mixed numbers**.

When we add a whole number and a fraction, the result is a mixed number.

1. Write a mixed number for each of the following.

(a)

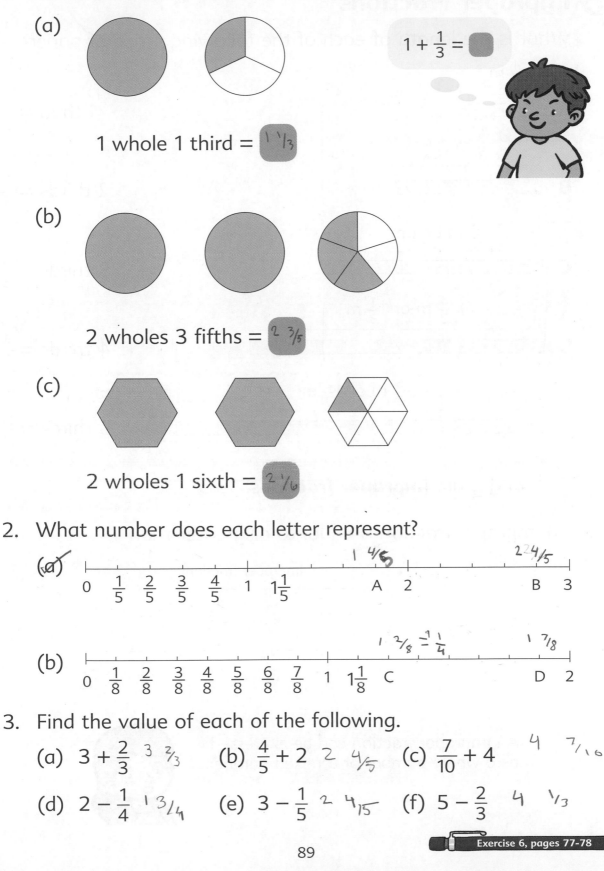

$1 + \dfrac{1}{3} = \boxed{}$

1 whole 1 third = $1\frac{1}{3}$

(b)

2 wholes 3 fifths = $2\frac{3}{5}$

(c)

2 wholes 1 sixth = $2\frac{1}{6}$

2. What number does each letter represent?

(a)

$1\frac{4}{5}$ $2\frac{4}{5}$

0   $\frac{1}{5}$ $\frac{2}{5}$ $\frac{3}{5}$ $\frac{4}{5}$ 1 $1\frac{1}{5}$ A   2   B   3

(b)

$1\frac{2}{8} = 1\frac{1}{4}$ $1\frac{7}{8}$

0   $\frac{1}{8}$ $\frac{2}{8}$ $\frac{3}{8}$ $\frac{4}{8}$ $\frac{5}{8}$ $\frac{6}{8}$ $\frac{7}{8}$ 1 $1\frac{1}{8}$ C   D   2

3. Find the value of each of the following.

(a) $3 + \dfrac{2}{3}$ $3\frac{2}{3}$ (b) $\dfrac{4}{5} + 2$ $2\frac{4}{5}$ (c) $\dfrac{7}{10} + 4$ $4\frac{7}{10}$

(d) $2 - \dfrac{1}{4}$ $1\frac{3}{4}$ (e) $3 - \dfrac{1}{5}$ $2\frac{4}{5}$ (f) $5 - \dfrac{2}{3}$ $4\frac{1}{3}$

89

Exercise 6, pages 77-78

④ Improper Fractions

What is the length of each of the following strips of paper?

$\frac{1}{3}$ m

A

1 third = $\frac{1}{3}$

$\frac{2}{3}$ m

B

2 thirds = $\frac{2}{3}$

$\frac{3}{3}$ m or 1 m

C

3 thirds = $\frac{3}{3}$

$\frac{4}{3}$ m or $1\frac{1}{3}$ m

D

4 thirds = $\frac{4}{3}$

$\frac{5}{3}$ m or $1\frac{2}{3}$ m

E

5 thirds = $\frac{5}{3}$

$\frac{3}{3}$, $\frac{4}{3}$, and $\frac{5}{3}$ are **improper fractions**.

An improper fraction is equal to or greater than 1.

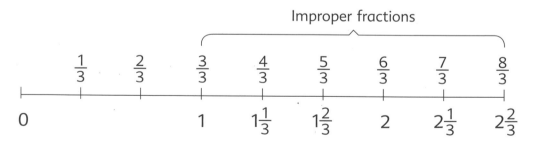

Improper fractions

$\frac{1}{3}$ $\frac{2}{3}$ $\frac{3}{3}$ $\frac{4}{3}$ $\frac{5}{3}$ $\frac{6}{3}$ $\frac{7}{3}$ $\frac{8}{3}$

0   1 $1\frac{1}{3}$ $1\frac{2}{3}$ 2 $2\frac{1}{3}$ $2\frac{2}{3}$

An improper fraction can be expressed as a whole number or a mixed number.

90

1. How many halves are there in $3\frac{1}{2}$?

$$3\frac{1}{2} = \frac{7}{2}$$

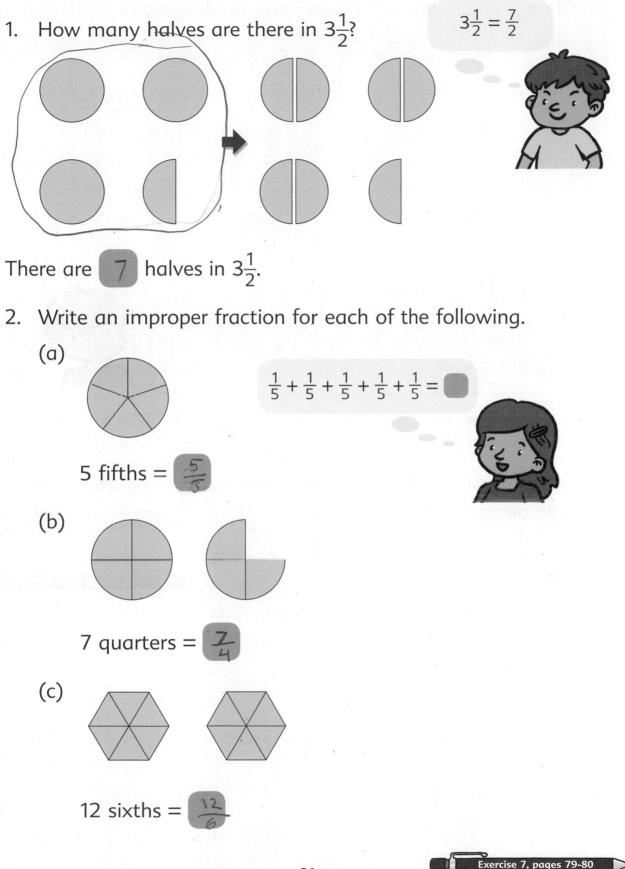

There are 7 halves in $3\frac{1}{2}$.

2. Write an improper fraction for each of the following.

(a)

$$\frac{1}{5} + \frac{1}{5} + \frac{1}{5} + \frac{1}{5} + \frac{1}{5} = \boxed{}$$

5 fifths = $\frac{5}{5}$

(b)

7 quarters = $\frac{7}{4}$

(c)

12 sixths = $\frac{12}{6}$

91

Exercise 7, pages 79-80

3. Change the improper fractions to mixed numbers.

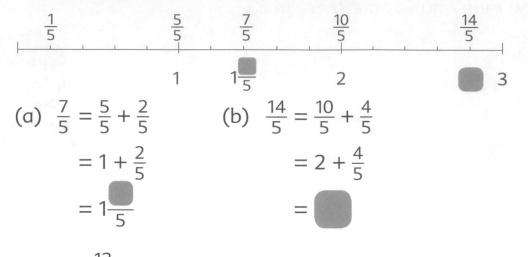

(a) $\dfrac{7}{5} = \dfrac{5}{5} + \dfrac{2}{5}$

$= 1 + \dfrac{2}{5}$

$= 1\dfrac{\boxed{}}{5}$

(b) $\dfrac{14}{5} = \dfrac{10}{5} + \dfrac{4}{5}$

$= 2 + \dfrac{4}{5}$

$= \boxed{}$

4. Change $\dfrac{13}{6}$ to a mixed number.

$\dfrac{13}{6} = \dfrac{12}{6} + \dfrac{1}{6}$

$= 2 + \dfrac{1}{6}$

$= \boxed{}$

$\dfrac{6}{6} = 1$

$\dfrac{12}{6} = 2$

5. Express each of the following as a mixed number or a whole number.

(a) $\dfrac{17}{4}$ (b) $\dfrac{10}{3}$ (c) $\dfrac{8}{2}$ (d) $\dfrac{12}{5}$

Exercise 8, pages 81-82

6. Change the mixed numbers to improper fractions.

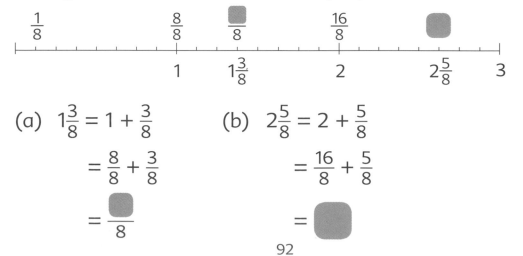

(a) $1\dfrac{3}{8} = 1 + \dfrac{3}{8}$

$= \dfrac{8}{8} + \dfrac{3}{8}$

$= \dfrac{\boxed{}}{8}$

(b) $2\dfrac{5}{8} = 2 + \dfrac{5}{8}$

$= \dfrac{16}{8} + \dfrac{5}{8}$

$= \boxed{}$

7. Change $3\frac{1}{6}$ into an improper fraction.

$$3\frac{1}{6} = 3 + \frac{1}{6}$$

$$= \frac{18}{6} + \frac{1}{6}$$

$$= \boxed{}$$

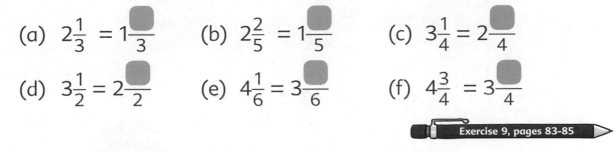

$$1 = \frac{6}{6}$$

$$3 = \frac{18}{6}$$

8. Express each of the following as an improper fraction.

  (a) $1\frac{4}{5}$ (b) $2\frac{2}{3}$ (c) $2\frac{1}{4}$ (d) $2\frac{5}{6}$

9. Find the missing numerator in each of the following.

  (a) $2\frac{1}{3} = 1\frac{\boxed{}}{3}$ (b) $2\frac{2}{5} = 1\frac{\boxed{}}{5}$ (c) $3\frac{1}{4} = 2\frac{\boxed{}}{4}$

  (d) $3\frac{1}{2} = 2\frac{\boxed{}}{2}$ (e) $4\frac{1}{6} = 3\frac{\boxed{}}{6}$ (f) $4\frac{3}{4} = 3\frac{\boxed{}}{4}$

Exercise 9, pages 83-85

10. Express each of the following as a whole number or a mixed number in its simplest form.

  (a) $\frac{10}{4}$ (b) $\frac{12}{3}$ (c) $2\frac{5}{10}$ (d) $2\frac{8}{12}$

  (e) $2\frac{8}{5}$ (f) $3\frac{7}{4}$ (g) $1\frac{6}{8}$ (h) $2\frac{6}{3}$

11. Add. Give each answer in its simplest form.

  (a) $\frac{5}{6} + \frac{5}{6}$ (b) $\frac{3}{5} + \frac{4}{5}$ (c) $\frac{3}{4} + \frac{1}{4}$

  (d) $\frac{6}{7} + \frac{5}{7}$ (e) $\frac{7}{10} + \frac{4}{5}$ (f) $\frac{7}{8} + \frac{3}{4}$

12. Subtract. Give each answer in its simplest form.

  (a) $3 - \frac{3}{4}$ (b) $2 - \frac{3}{8}$ (c) $4 - \frac{1}{2}$

  (d) $2 - \frac{3}{10}$ (e) $2 - \frac{4}{5}$ (f) $3 - \frac{5}{7}$

Exercise 10, pages 86-87

⑤ Fractions and Division

Share 2 cakes equally among 3 children. Each child receives 2 thirds.

$$2 \div 3 = \frac{2}{3}$$

Share 5 cakes equally among 3 children. Each child receives 5 thirds.

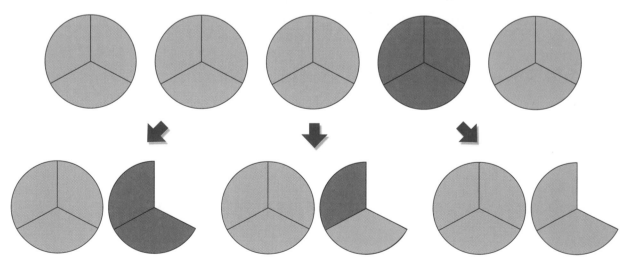

$$5 \div 3 = \frac{5}{3}$$

Here is another way to divide 5 by 3.

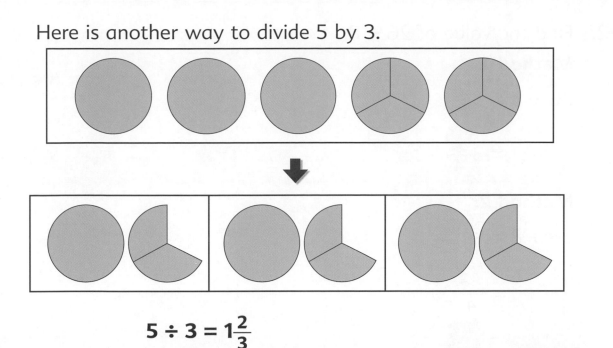

$$5 \div 3 = 1\frac{2}{3}$$

$$\begin{array}{r} 1 \\ 3\overline{)5} \\ 3 \\ \hline 2 \end{array}$$

$1\frac{2}{3}$ is the same as $\frac{5}{3}$.

1. A ribbon, 7 m long, is cut into 2 equal pieces.
   What is the length of each piece?

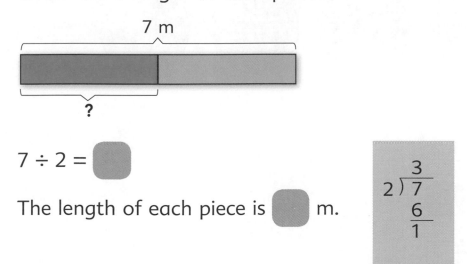

$$7 \div 2 = \boxed{}$$

The length of each piece is $\boxed{}$ m.

$$\begin{array}{r} 3 \\ 2\overline{)7} \\ 6 \\ \hline 1 \end{array}$$

2. Find the value of $26 \div 8$.

   Method 1:

   $$26 \div 8 = 3\frac{2}{8}$$

   $$= 3\frac{\boxed{}}{4}$$

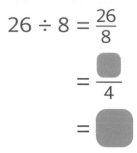

   Method 2:

   $$26 \div 8 = \frac{26}{8}$$

   $$= \frac{\boxed{}}{4}$$

   $$= \boxed{}$$

3. Find the value of

   (a) $9 \div 4$ (b) $13 \div 5$ (c) $20 \div 6$

4. Express $\frac{15}{4}$ as a mixed number.

   Method 1:

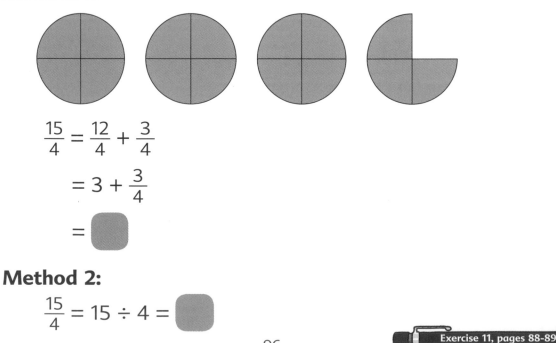

   $$\frac{15}{4} = \frac{12}{4} + \frac{3}{4}$$

   $$= 3 + \frac{3}{4}$$

   $$= \boxed{}$$

   Method 2:

   $$\frac{15}{4} = 15 \div 4 = \boxed{}$$

Exercise 11, pages 88-89

PRACTICE C

1. Express each of the following as an improper fraction.

   (a) $1\frac{2}{5}$ (b) $1\frac{1}{9}$ (c) $2\frac{2}{3}$ (d) $2\frac{2}{9}$

   (e) $3\frac{5}{6}$ (f) $2\frac{5}{8}$ (g) $2\frac{7}{10}$ (h) $3\frac{7}{12}$

2. Express each of the following as a whole number or a mixed number in its simplest form.

   (a) $\frac{14}{5}$ (b) $\frac{20}{4}$ (c) $\frac{15}{8}$ (d) $\frac{21}{6}$

   (e) $\frac{30}{10}$ (f) $\frac{18}{3}$ (g) $\frac{20}{9}$ (h) $\frac{9}{6}$

   (i) $3\frac{6}{8}$ (j) $2\frac{7}{4}$ (k) $2\frac{15}{10}$ (l) $2\frac{5}{5}$

3. Mr. Kent mixed 2 gallons of white paint with $\frac{3}{4}$ gallons of black paint to get gray paint. How much gray paint did he get?

4. Mrs. Parker baked 2 cakes of the same size. She gave $\frac{1}{2}$ of a cake to her sister. How much cake did she have left?

5. A box of apples weighing 3 pounds was divided into 6 equal shares. What was the weight of each share in pounds?

6. Mary cut a ribbon into 4 equal pieces. If the ribbon was 6 m long, how many meters long was each piece?

6 Fraction of a Set

2 out of 5 children are girls.
What fraction of the children are girls?

2 out of 5 groups of children are made up of girls.
What fraction of the children are girls?

2 out of 5 is $\frac{2}{5}$.

1. What fraction of each set is shaded?

(a)

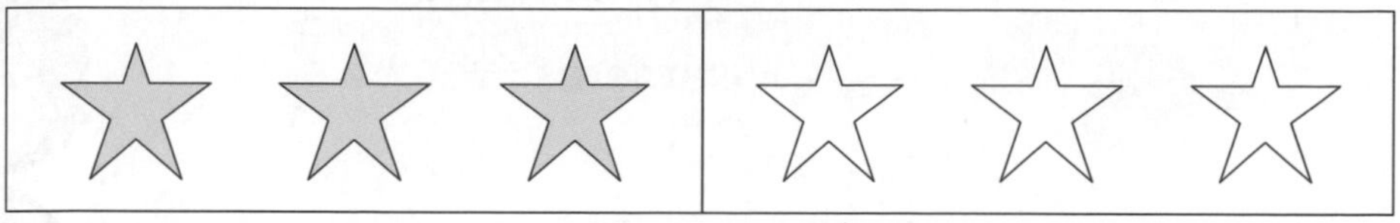

(b)

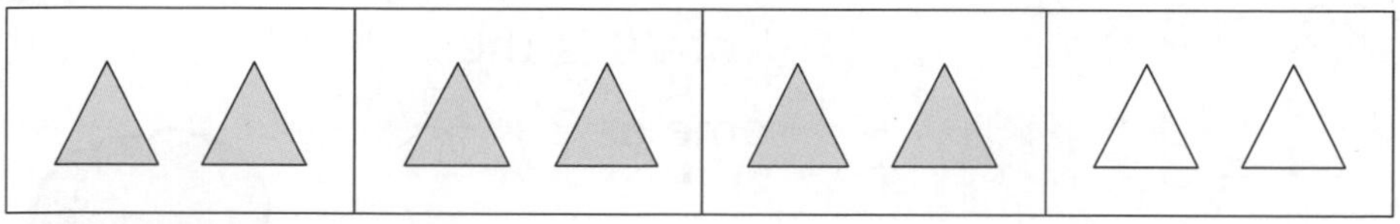

(c)

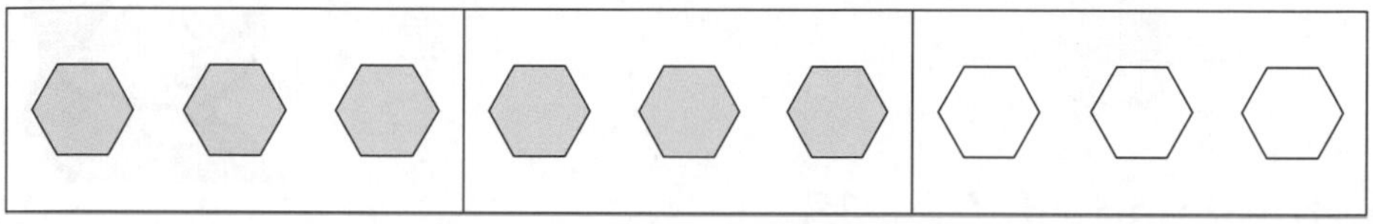

(d)

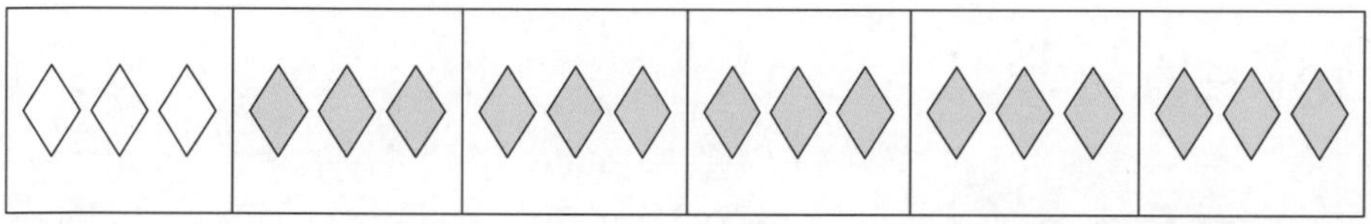

Exercise 12, pages 90-92

2. What is $\frac{1}{3}$ of 12?

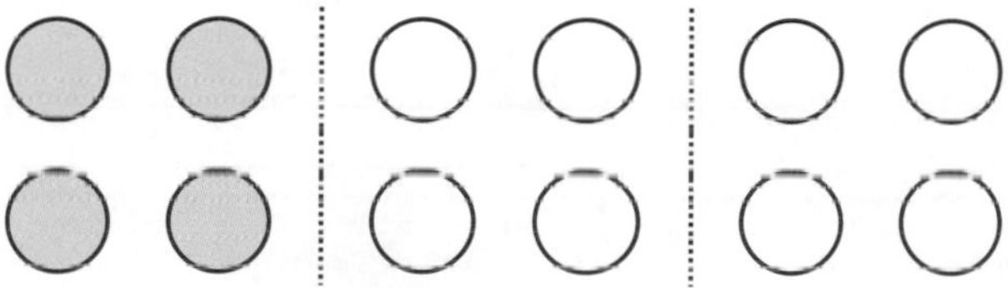

$\frac{1}{3}$ of 12 = ▢

Divide 12 into 3 equal groups.
One group is $\frac{1}{3}$ of 12.
$\frac{1}{3}$ of 12 is 4.

3. Find the value of $\frac{3}{4}$ of 20.

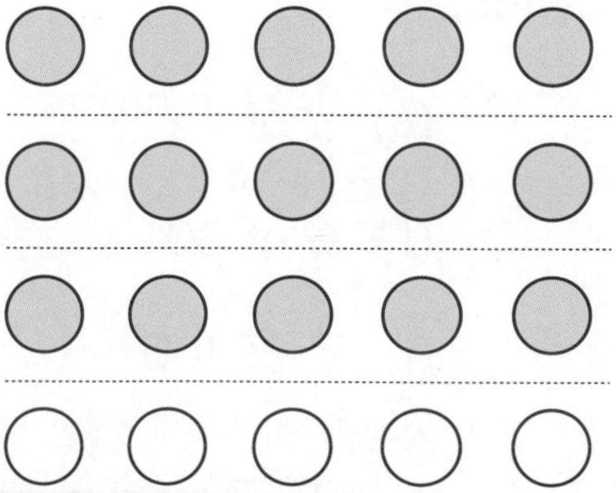

$\frac{1}{4}$ of 20 = ▢

$\frac{3}{4}$ of 20 = ▢

99

Exercise 13, pages 93-94

$\frac{1}{4}$ of 20 $= \frac{20}{4}$

$\qquad = \boxed{}$

$\frac{1}{4}$ of 20 is the same as $\frac{20}{4}$.

$\frac{3}{4}$ of 20 $= 3 \times \frac{20}{4}$

$\qquad = 3 \times \boxed{}$

$\qquad = \boxed{}$

$\frac{3}{4}$ of 20 is the same as $3 \times \frac{20}{4}$.

4. Find the value of $\frac{5}{6}$ of 18.

$\frac{5}{6}$ of 18 $= 5 \times \frac{18}{6}$

$\qquad = 5 \times \boxed{}$

$\qquad = \boxed{}$

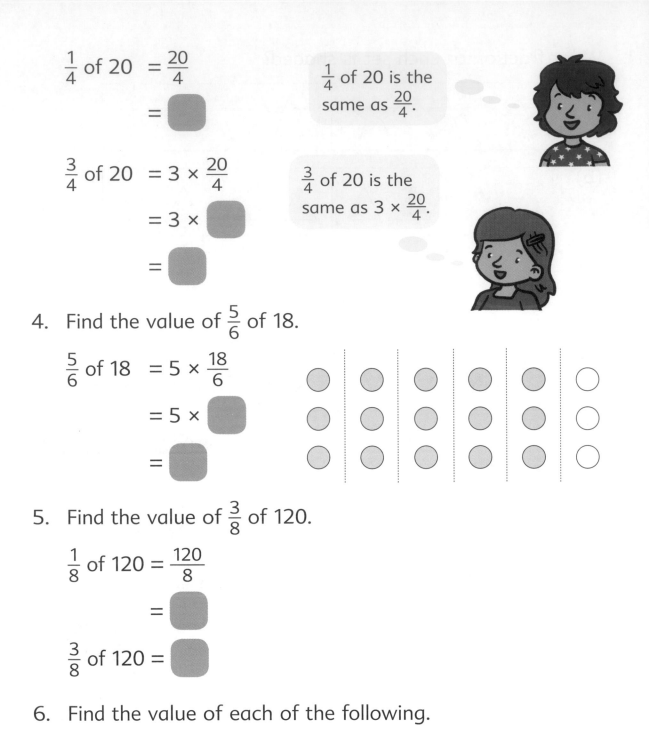

5. Find the value of $\frac{3}{8}$ of 120.

$\frac{1}{8}$ of 120 $= \frac{120}{8}$

$\qquad = \boxed{}$

$\frac{3}{8}$ of 120 $= \boxed{}$

6. Find the value of each of the following.

(a) $\frac{1}{2}$ of 12

(b) $\frac{1}{5}$ of 20

(c) $\frac{1}{6}$ of 4

(d) $\frac{2}{3}$ of 9

(e) $\frac{3}{8}$ of 16

(f) $\frac{2}{3}$ of 30

(g) $\frac{1}{4}$ of 100

(h) $\frac{3}{4}$ of 100

(i) $\frac{3}{5}$ of 100

Exercise 14, pages 95-97

7. There are 8 coins.
6 of them are dimes.
What fraction of the coins are dimes?

6 out of 8 is $\frac{6}{8}$.

$\frac{\overset{3}{\cancel{6}}}{\underset{4}{\cancel{8}}} = \frac{3}{4}$

2 is a common factor of 6 and 8.
Divide 6 and 8 by 2:
$\frac{\cancel{6}^{3}}{\cancel{8}_{4}}$

☐ of the coins are dimes.

8. Matthew had 42 pebbles. He lost 6 of them.
What fraction of the pebbles did he lose?

$\frac{6}{42} = $ ☐

6 out of 42 is $\frac{6}{42}$.
Express $\frac{6}{42}$ in its simplest form.

He lost ☐ of the pebbles.

9. Jenny's handspan is 16 cm.
What fraction of 1 m is 16 cm?

$\frac{16}{100} = $ ☐

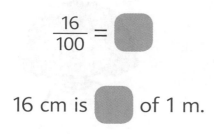

16 cm is ☐ of 1 m.

1 m = 100 cm

Exercise 15, pages 98-99

10. Kelley buys 24 flowers. $\frac{2}{3}$ of them are white.

    How many white flowers are there?

    Method 1:

    > Divide 24 into 3 equal parts.
    > 24 = 3 units
    > $\frac{2}{3}$ of 24 = 2 units

    3 units = 24

    1 unit   = ⬜

    2 units = ⬜

    There are ⬜ white flowers.

    > $\frac{2}{3}$ of 24 is the same as $2 \times \frac{24}{3}$.

    Method 2:

    $\frac{2}{3} \times 24 =$ ⬜

    There are ⬜ white flowers.

Exercise 16, pages 100–101

11. Alice had $20.

    She used $\frac{2}{5}$ of it to buy a book.

    How much did she have left?

    Method 1:

    $$\frac{2}{5} \times 20 = 2 \times \frac{20}{5}$$
    $$= 8$$

    > First, I find the amount of money she used.

    She used $8.

    $20 - 8 =$ ⬜

    She had $⬜ left.

Method 2:

$$1 - \frac{2}{5} = \frac{3}{5}$$

She had $\frac{3}{5}$ of her money left.

$$\frac{3}{5} \times 20 = \boxed{}$$

She had $\boxed{}$ left.

First, I find what fraction of the money is left.

Method 3:

$20

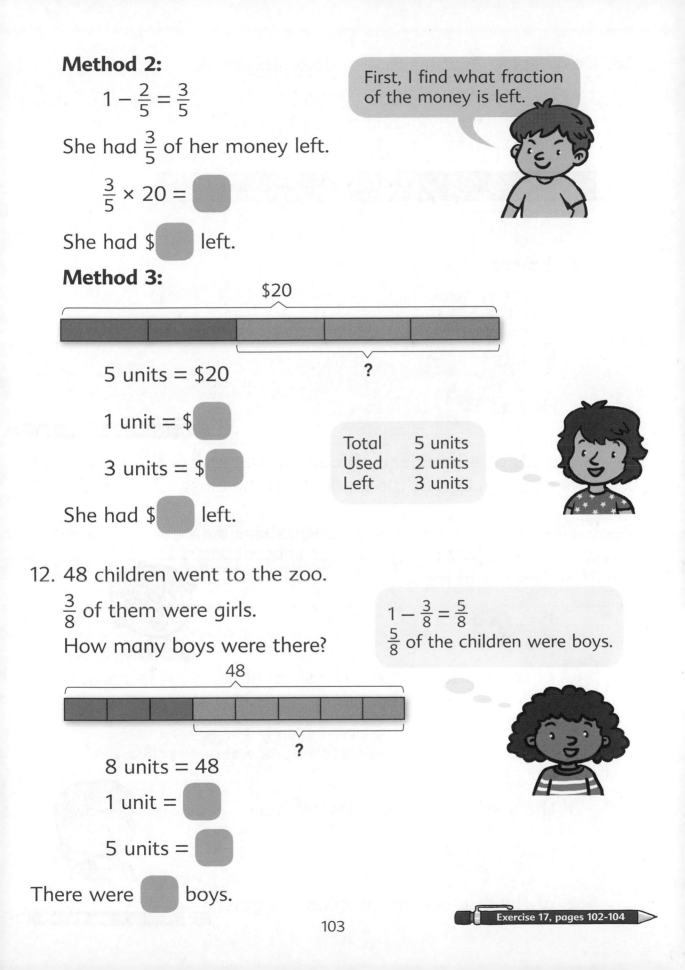

5 units = $20

?

1 unit = $\boxed{}$

3 units = $\boxed{}$

She had $\boxed{}$ left.

Total   5 units
Used   2 units
Left   3 units

12. 48 children went to the zoo.
$\frac{3}{8}$ of them were girls.
How many boys were there?

$$1 - \frac{3}{8} = \frac{5}{8}$$
$\frac{5}{8}$ of the children were boys.

48

?

8 units = 48

1 unit = $\boxed{}$

5 units = $\boxed{}$

There were $\boxed{}$ boys.

Exercise 17, pages 102-104

13. David spent $\frac{2}{5}$ of his money on a storybook.

The storybook cost $20.
How much money did he have at first?

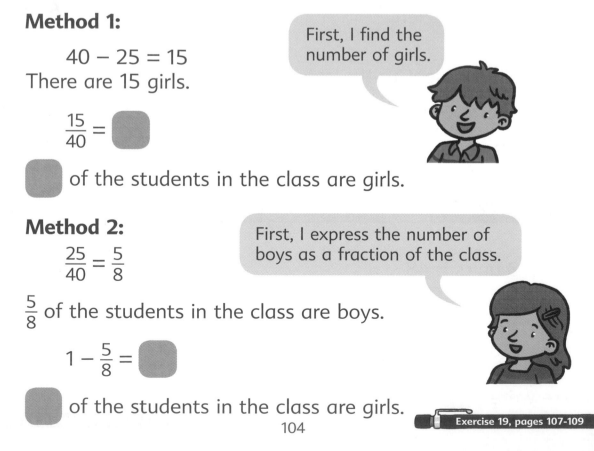

?

$20

2 units = $20

1 unit = $ ☐

5 units = $ ☐

He had $ ☐ at first.

Exercise 18, pages 105-106

14. In a class of 40 students, 25 are boys. Express the number of girls as a fraction of the students in the class.

Method 1:

First, I find the number of girls.

$40 - 25 = 15$
There are 15 girls.

$\frac{15}{40} = $ ☐

☐ of the students in the class are girls.

Method 2:

First, I express the number of boys as a fraction of the class.

$\frac{25}{40} = \frac{5}{8}$

$\frac{5}{8}$ of the students in the class are boys.

$1 - \frac{5}{8} = $ ☐

☐ of the students in the class are girls.

Exercise 19, pages 107-109

Find the value of each of the following. Give each answer in its simplest form.

	(a)	(b)	(c)	(d)
1.	$\frac{1}{3}$ of 18	$\frac{3}{4}$ of 32	$\frac{1}{6}$ of 6	$\frac{5}{9}$ of 72
2.	$\frac{1}{2}$ of 100	$\frac{2}{5}$ of 100	$\frac{1}{8}$ of 180	$\frac{3}{4}$ of 1000

3. Peter had a board 3 m long. He used $\frac{3}{4}$ of its length as a bookshelf. How long was the bookshelf?

4. Jane practices on the piano for $\frac{3}{4}$ of an hour a day. How many minutes does she practice each day?

5. In a class, $\frac{2}{5}$ of the students wear glasses.
   (a) What fraction of the students do **not** wear glasses?
   (b) If 16 students wear glasses, how many students are there altogether?

6. Nicole bought 30 eggs. She used $\frac{2}{3}$ of the eggs to bake cakes. How many eggs did she have left?

7. Lily bought some picture cards. She gave $\frac{1}{3}$ of them to Matthew. If she gave 8 picture cards to Matthew, how many picture cards did she buy?

8. Kevin spent $\frac{1}{4}$ of his money on a storybook. If the storybook cost $6, how much money did he have at first?

1. Write the following in figures.
    (a) seven thousand, three
    (b) fifteen thousand, two hundred twelve
    (c) sixty-two million, four hundred nine thousand, two hundred
    (d) negative forty-seven

2. Write the following in words.
    (a) 46,600   (b) 356,000   (c) 470,019   (d) 502,473

3. Arrange the numbers in increasing order.
    (a) 74,355,   75,435,   47,355,   74,535
    (b) 32,223,   33,222,   23,322,   23,232
    (c) 30, −10, 0, 2, −5, 20

4. (a) What number is 100 more than 15,960?
    (b) What number is 1000 less than 70,516?
    (c) What number is 1 less than −100?
    (d) What number is 1 more than −100?

5. The continental shelf slopes downward to a depth of about 200 m. Write this as a number, with sea level at 0 m.

6. Round each number to the nearest thousand.
    (a) 41,300   (b) 68,500   (c) 596,800

7. Round each number to the nearest hundred thousand.
    (a) 683,000 (b) 5,608,000 (c) 7,449,000

8. (a) Find the sum of 4786 and 599.
    (b) Find the difference between 2976 and 5076.
    (c) Find the product of 15 and 306.
    (d) Find the quotient and remainder when 3650 is divided by 8.

9. Find the missing factor represented by *f* in each of the following equations.
   (a) $45 = 5 \times f$
   (b) $16 = 2 \times f$
   (c) $27 = f \times 9$
   (d) $18 = f \times 9$
   (e) $45 \times 3 = 5 \times f \times 3$
   (f) $16 \times 7 = 2 \times f \times 7$
   (g) $4 \times 27 = 4 \times f \times 9$
   (h) $2 \times 48 = 2 \times f \times 24$

10. What are the prime numbers between 10 and 20?

11. Find the value of each expression.

    (a) $(4 + 32) \div 6 + 15$
    (b) $1000 - (20 \times 100 \div 8)$

12. Add or subtract. Give each answer in its simplest form.

    (a) $\frac{1}{3} + \frac{5}{12}$
    (b) $\frac{4}{9} + \frac{1}{3}$

    (c) $\frac{1}{12} + \frac{5}{6}$
    (d) $\frac{1}{2} - \frac{3}{10}$

    (e) $\frac{2}{3} - \frac{5}{12}$
    (f) $\frac{7}{8} - \frac{3}{4}$

13. What fraction of each figure is shaded?
    Give each answer in its simplest form.

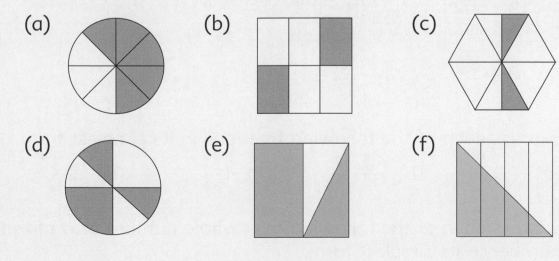

(a)   (b)   (c)

(d)   (e)   (f)

14. What fraction of each set is shaded?
    Give each answer in its simplest form.

    (a)

    (b)

    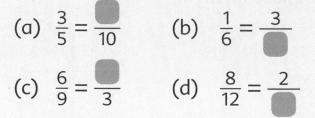

15. Arrange the numbers in increasing order.

    $\frac{4}{4}$ $\frac{3}{5}$ $\frac{1}{3}$ $\frac{3}{2}$ $\frac{1}{12}$

16. Find the missing numerator or denominator.

    (a) $\frac{3}{5} = \frac{\blacksquare}{10}$ (b) $\frac{1}{6} = \frac{3}{\blacksquare}$

    (c) $\frac{6}{9} = \frac{\blacksquare}{3}$ (d) $\frac{8}{12} = \frac{2}{\blacksquare}$

17. Express each of the following fractions in its simplest form.

    (a) $\frac{8}{10}$ (b) $\frac{2}{12}$ (c) $1\frac{2}{6}$ (d) $2\frac{3}{12}$

18. Express each of the following as a whole number or a mixed
    number in its simplest form.

    (a) $\frac{10}{3}$ (b) $\frac{15}{5}$ (c) $\frac{18}{4}$ (d) $\frac{23}{7}$

19. Express each of the following as an improper fraction.

   (a) $1\frac{4}{7}$ (b) $2\frac{4}{5}$ (c) $3\frac{1}{8}$ (d) $2\frac{9}{10}$

20. A rope 18 m long is cut into 4 equal pieces. What is the length of each piece in meters? Give your answer as a mixed number in its simplest form.

21. Loraine bought a bottle of olive oil.
    She used $\frac{3}{10}$ of the oil.
    If she used 150 g of oil, how much oil did she buy?

22. Jordan poured 20 liters of water into an empty fish tank.
    If $\frac{5}{6}$ of the fish tank was filled, find the capacity of the tank.

23. Jennifer made 100 sandwiches for a children's party.
    The children ate $\frac{3}{4}$ of the sandwiches.
    How many sandwiches were left?

24.

    Lily bought these items at half of the given prices.
    How much did she spend altogether?

25. $\frac{4}{5}$ of the children in a choir are girls.

   (a) What fraction of the children are boys?
   (b) If there are 8 boys, how many children are there in the choir?
   (c) How many more girls than boys are there in the choir?

Review 3, pages 110-116

4 GEOMETRY

 Right Angles

Turning through 1 right angle (a $\frac{1}{4}$-turn)

Turning through 2 right angles (a $\frac{1}{2}$-turn)

Turning through 3 right angles (a $\frac{3}{4}$-turn)

Turning through 4 right angles (a complete turn)

$\frac{1}{4}$ of a complete turn is 1 right angle.

$\frac{1}{2}$ of a complete turn is 2 right angles.

$\frac{3}{4}$ of a complete turn is 3 right angles.

A complete turn is 4 right angles.

1. Fold a piece of paper twice to make a right angle.

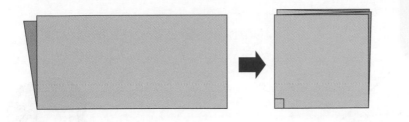

We mark a right angle like this:

2. Use a set-square to draw a right angle.

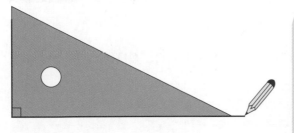

An **acute angle** is an angle that is smaller than a right angle. An **obtuse angle** is an angle that is greater than a right angle, but smaller than two right angles.

3. Which of the following angles are right angles?
   Which are acute angles?
   Which are obtuse angles?

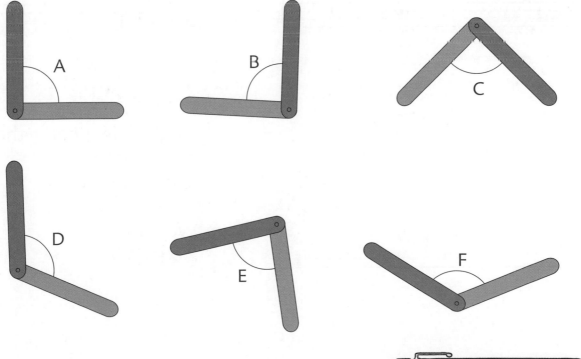

Exercise 1, pages 117-120

② Measuring Angles

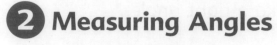

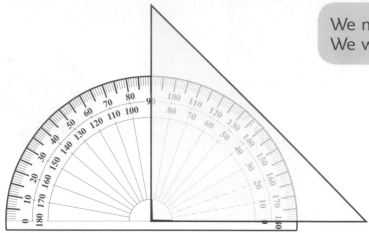

We measure angles in **degrees**.
We write 90° for 90 degrees.

1 right angle = 90°

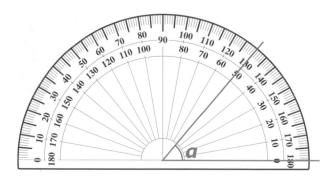

Angle *a* is smaller than a right angle.
It is 50 degrees.

We write:
∠*a* = 50°

Angle *b* is greater than a right angle.
It is 100 degrees.

We write:
∠*b* = 100°

1. What is the size of each angle?

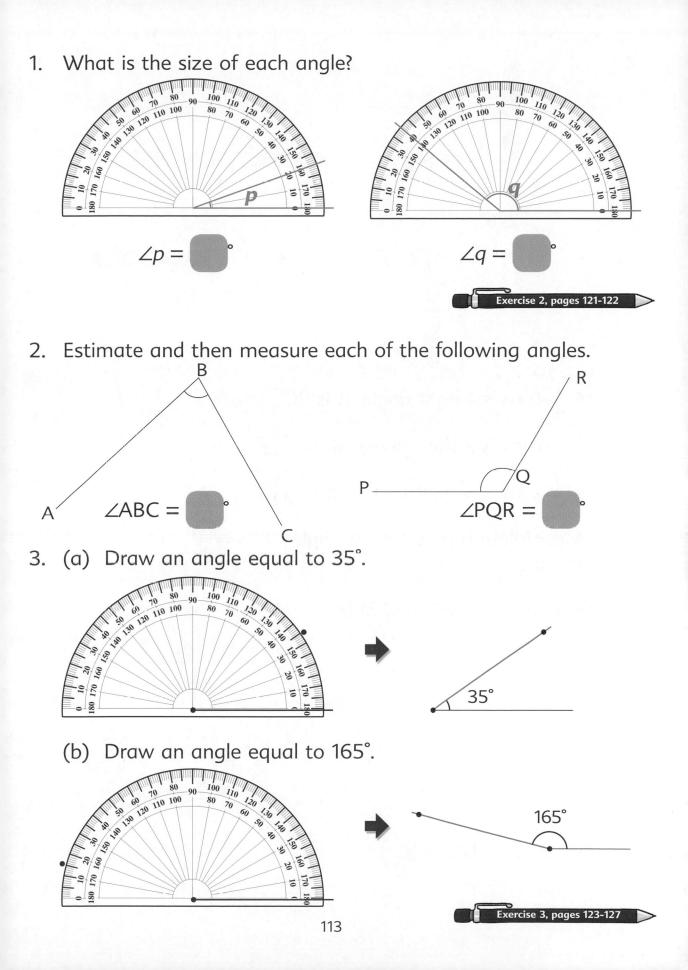

∠p = ◻°

∠q = ◻°

Exercise 2, pages 121-122

2. Estimate and then measure each of the following angles.

∠ABC = ◻°

∠PQR = ◻°

3. (a) Draw an angle equal to 35°.

35°

(b) Draw an angle equal to 165°.

165°

Exercise 3, pages 123-127

113

4.

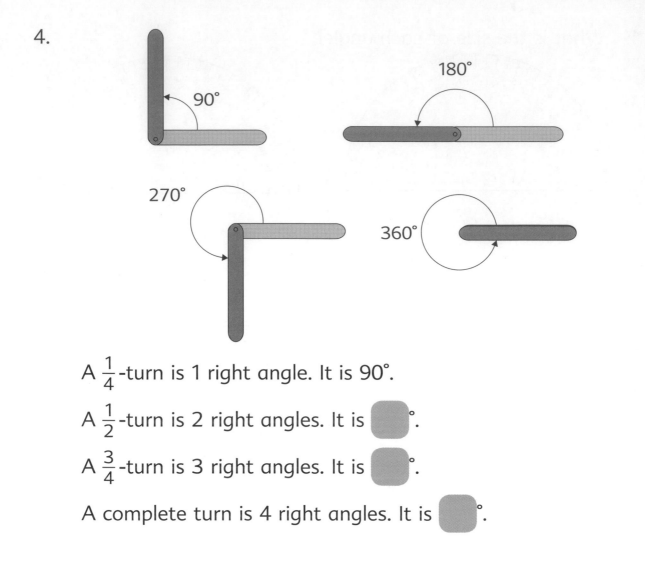

A $\frac{1}{4}$-turn is 1 right angle. It is 90°.

A $\frac{1}{2}$-turn is 2 right angles. It is ____°.

A $\frac{3}{4}$-turn is 3 right angles. It is ____°.

A complete turn is 4 right angles. It is ____°.

5. $\angle x$ is between 180° and 360°.

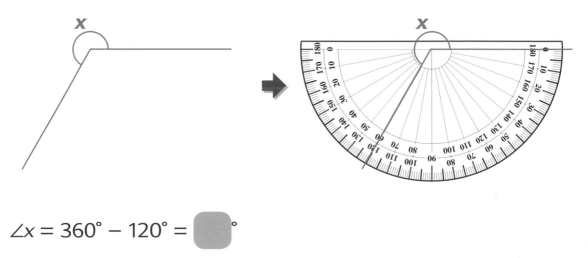

$\angle x = 360° - 120° =$ ____°

6. ∠y is between 270° and 360°.

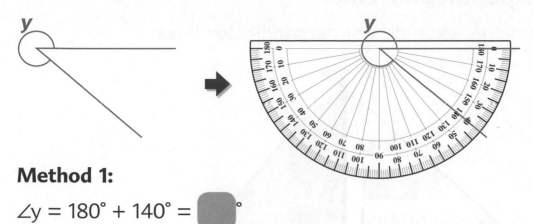

Method 1:

∠y = 180° + 140° = [ ]°

Method 2:

∠y = 360° − 40° = [ ]°

7. Draw an angle equal to 210°.

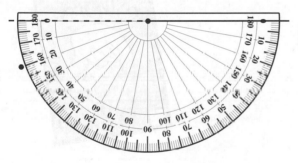

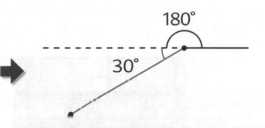

180° + 30° = 210°又

8. Measure these angles.

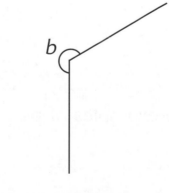

115

Exercise 4, pages 128-131

③ Perpendicular Lines

These are examples of **perpendicular lines**.

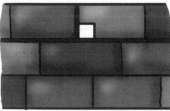

We mark a right angle to show a perpendicular line.

Look for some more examples of perpendicular lines around you.

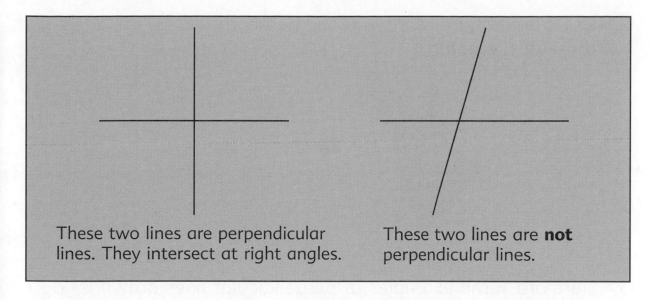

These two lines are perpendicular lines. They intersect at right angles.

These two lines are **not** perpendicular lines.

We can use a set-square to check for perpendicular lines.

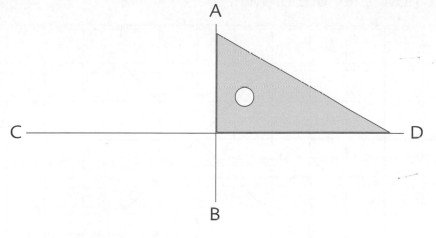

AB is perpendicular to CD.
We write: **AB ⊥ CD**.

1. How many pairs of perpendicular lines are there in each figure? Name each pair of perpendicular lines.

(a)

(b)

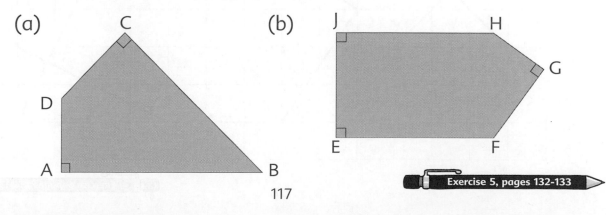

Exercise 5, pages 132-133

2. Use a set-square to draw a line perpendicular to the line AB through the point P.

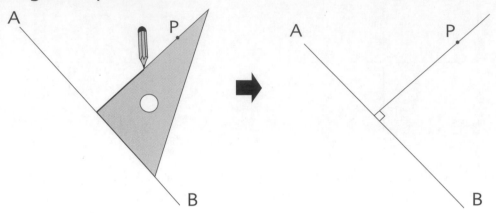

3. Here are some examples of perpendicular lines drawn on a square grid.
   Find out how they are drawn.

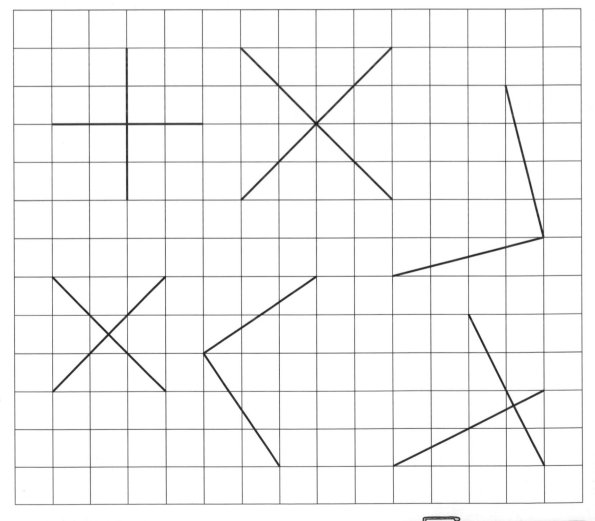

Exercise 6, pages 134-135

Parallel Lines

These are examples of **parallel lines**.

We draw arrowheads to show parallel lines.

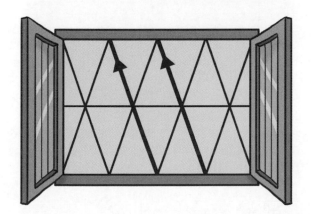

Look for some more examples of parallel lines around you.

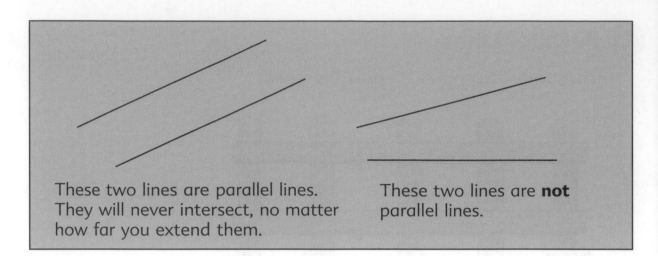

These two lines are parallel lines. They will never intersect, no matter how far you extend them.

These two lines are **not** parallel lines.

We can slide a set-square along a ruler to check for parallel lines.

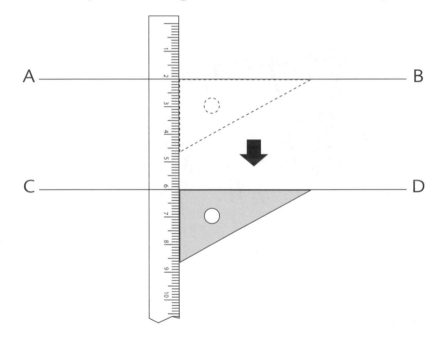

AB is parallel to CD.
We write: **AB // CD**.

1. In the 5-sided figure PQRST, which two sides are perpendicular to each other?
    Which two sides are parallel to each other?

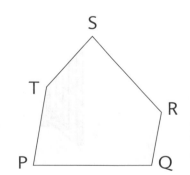

Exercise 7, pages 136-137

2. Use a set-square and a ruler to draw a line parallel to the line AB through the point P.

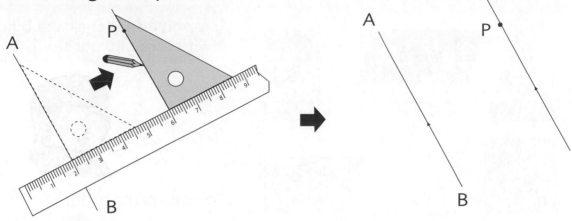

3. Here are some examples of parallel lines drawn on a square grid. Find out how they are drawn.

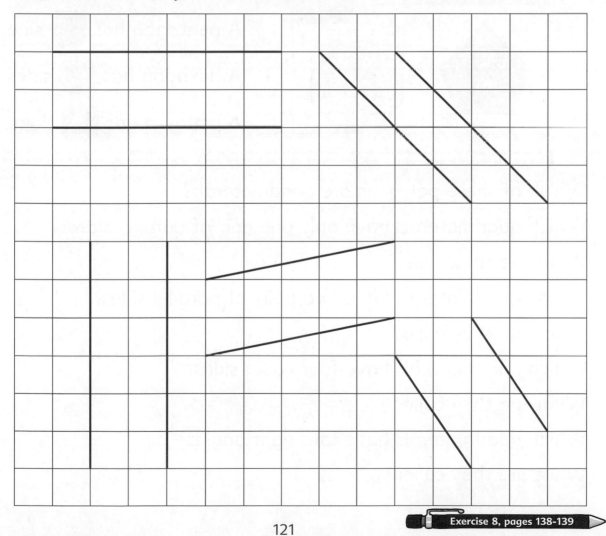

Exercise 8, pages 138-139

 **5 Quadrilaterals**

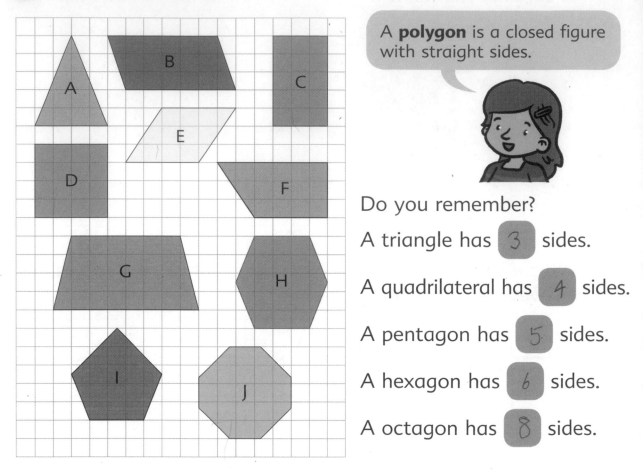

A **polygon** is a closed figure with straight sides.

Do you remember?

A triangle has 3 sides.

A quadrilateral has 4 sides.

A pentagon has 5 sides.

A hexagon has 6 sides.

A octagon has 8 sides.

Which of these polygons are quadrilaterals? G, D,E,B,C,F

Which quadrilaterals have only one pair of parallel sides? F G

What are they called? trapezoids

Which quadrilaterals have two pairs of parallel sides? B,C,D,E,

What are they called? parallelograms

Which quadrilaterals have four equal sides? C and E

What are they called? rhombus

Which quadrilaterals have four right angles? D and C

What are they called? rectangels

122

1. A trapezoid is a quadrilateral with **only one** pair of parallel sides.

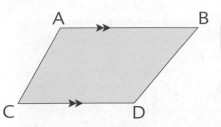

We draw arrowheads to mark which sides are parallel to each other.

Which two sides are parallel to each other?
Which angles are obtuse?
Which angles are acute?

2. A parallelogram is a quadrilateral with two pairs of parallel sides.

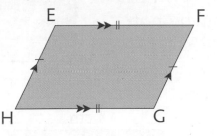

We draw lines to mark which sides are equal in length to each other.

Name each pair of parallel lines.
Name each pair of equal lines.

3. A rhombus is a parallelogram with equal sides.

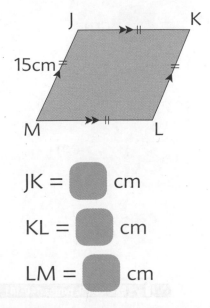

This is a scale drawing. It is smaller than the actual size.

JK = ⬜ cm

KL = ⬜ cm

LM = ⬜ cm

123

4. Figure WXYZ is a parallelogram with 4 right angles.

What is another name for this figure?
Name each pair of perpendicular sides.

$YZ = $ 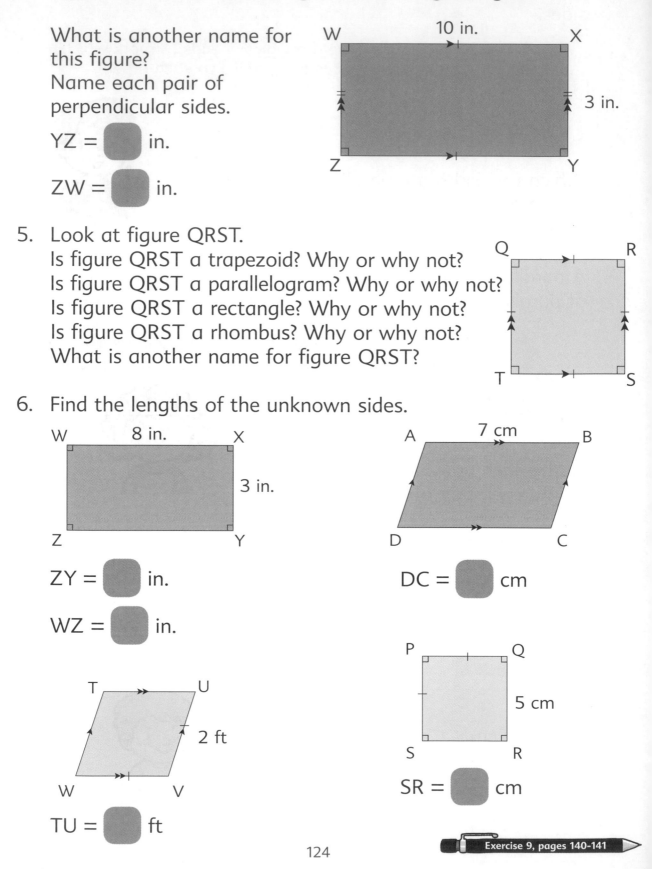 in.

$ZW = $ in.

W — 10 in. — X

3 in.

Z — Y

5. Look at figure QRST.
Is figure QRST a trapezoid? Why or why not?
Is figure QRST a parallelogram? Why or why not?
Is figure QRST a rectangle? Why or why not?
Is figure QRST a rhombus? Why or why not?
What is another name for figure QRST?

Q — R

T — S

6. Find the lengths of the unknown sides.

W — 8 in. — X

3 in.

Z — Y

$ZY = $ in.

$WZ = $ in.

A — 7 cm — B

D — C

$DC = $ cm

T — U

2 ft

W — V

$TU = $ ft

P — Q

5 cm

S — R

$SR = $ cm

124

6 Triangles

Courtney used straws of different lengths to make these triangles.

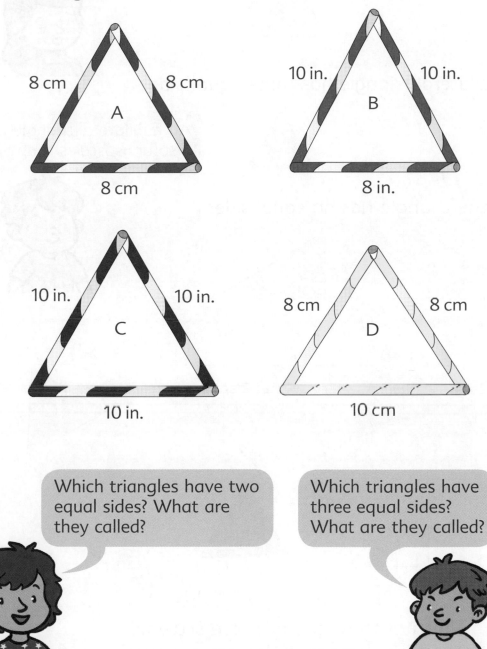

Which triangles have two equal sides? What are they called?

Which triangles have three equal sides? What are they called?

An isosceles triangle has two equal sides.

We mark equal sides.

An equilateral triangle has three equal sides.

An equilateral triangle is also an isosceles triangle.

A scalene triangle has no equal sides.

1.

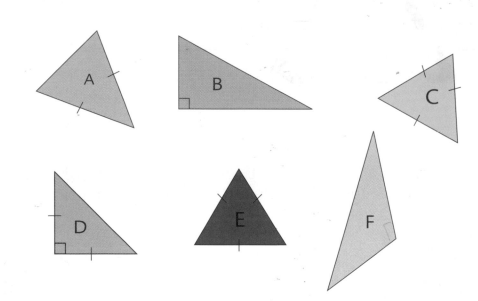

✓(a) Which of these triangles are scalene? F,B,
✓(b) Which of these triangles are isosceles? A,D (cE)
✓(c) Which of these triangles are equilateral? E,C,
✓(d) Which of these triangles have a right angle? B,D
✓(e) Which of these triangles have an obtuse angle? F
 (f) Can a triangle have two obtuse angles? No

2. Find the length of each unknown side.

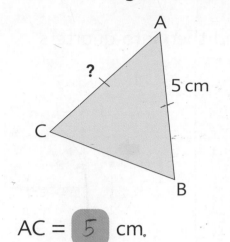

AC = 5 cm.

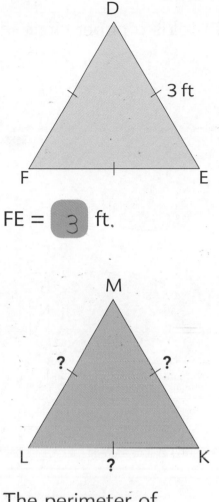

FE = 3 ft.

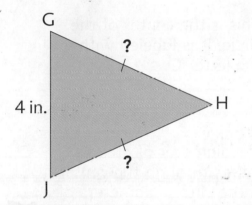

The perimeter of
figure GHJ is 22 in.

GH = 9 in.

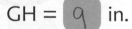

The perimeter of
figure KLM is 30 cm.

MK = 10 cm

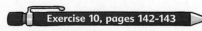

Exercise 10, pages 142-143

7 Circles

Mia folds a paper circle into half and then into quarters.

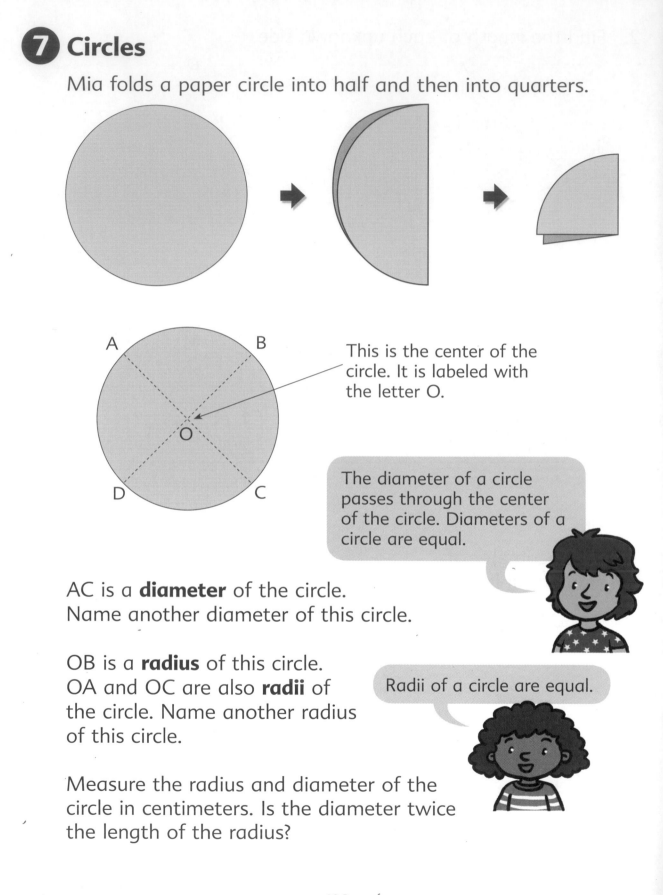

This is the center of the circle. It is labeled with the letter O.

The diameter of a circle passes through the center of the circle. Diameters of a circle are equal.

AC is a **diameter** of the circle.
Name another diameter of this circle.

OB is a **radius** of this circle.
OA and OC are also **radii** of the circle. Name another radius of this circle.

Radii of a circle are equal.

Measure the radius and diameter of the circle in centimeters. Is the diameter twice the length of the radius?

1. In this figure, O is the center of the circle.

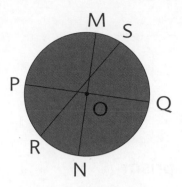

(a) Name the diameters. MN PQ
(b) Which line is not a diameter? Why not? RS It doesn't go through the center. The center
(c) If the radius of the circle is 6 cm, what is the diameter? 12 cm
(d) If the diameter of the circle is 8 inches, what is the radius? 4 cm

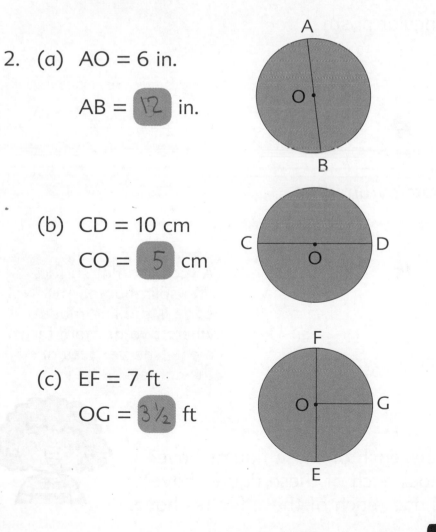

2. (a) AO = 6 in.

   AB = 12 in.

(b) CD = 10 cm

   CO = 5 cm

(c) EF = 7 ft

   OG = 3½ ft

Exercise 11, pages 144-145

8 Solid Figures

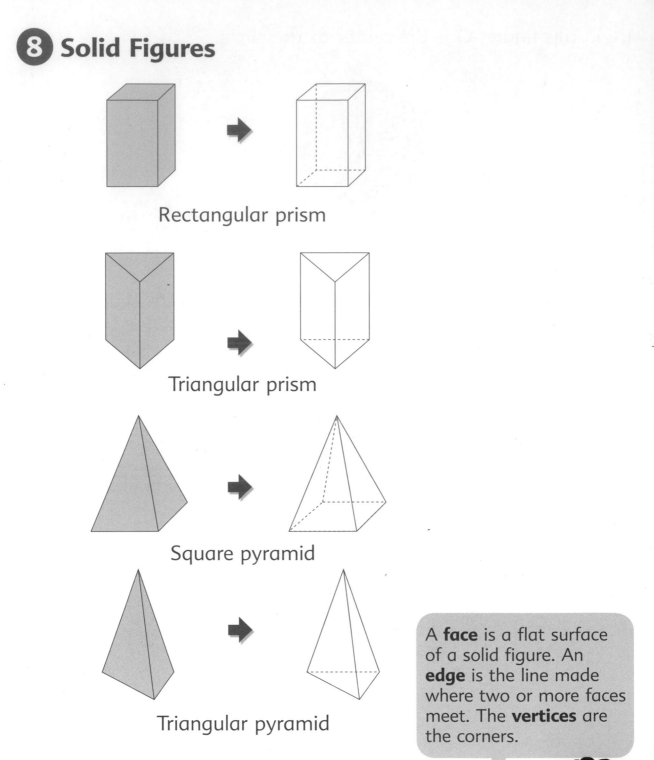

Rectangular prism

Triangular prism

Square pyramid

Triangular pyramid

A **face** is a flat surface of a solid figure. An **edge** is the line made where two or more faces meet. The **vertices** are the corners.

How many faces does each of these figures have?
How many edges does each of these figures have?
How many vertices does each of these figures have?

1. The figures below show some solids.
   Which one of the solids has a curved surface? *Cylinder*
   Does a cylinder have any faces? *yes 2*

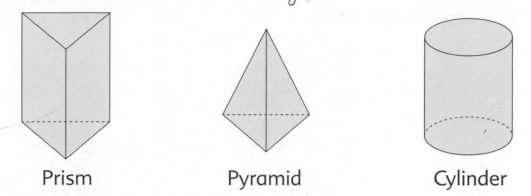

| Prism | Pyramid | Cylinder |

2. The figures below show some solids.
   How many faces of each solid are triangles? *2*
   How many faces of each solid are rectangles? *3*

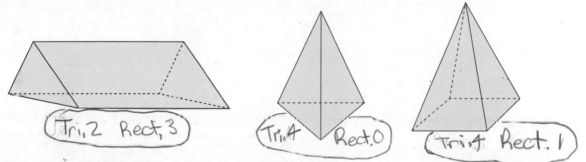

Tri. 2 Rect. 3   *Tri. 4 Rect. 0*   *Tri. 4 Rect. 1*

3. The figures below show some solids.
   Which one of the solids is different from the others? Explain
   why. *√*

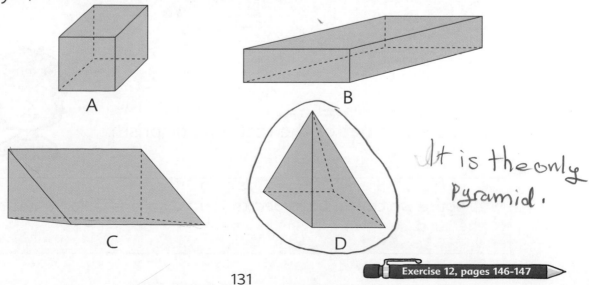

A

B

C

D

It is the only Pyramid.

Exercise 12, pages 146-147

Nets

Trace and cut out the figure. Fold it along the lines. You will get a rectangular prism.

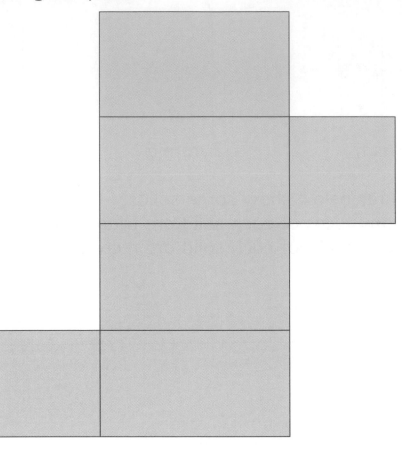

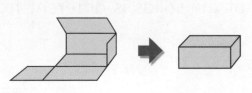

The figure is a **net** of the rectangular prism.

A figure which can be folded to form a solid is called a **net** of the solid.

1. Trace and cut out the figures below.
   Fold each figure along the lines to form a solid.

   (a)

   (b)

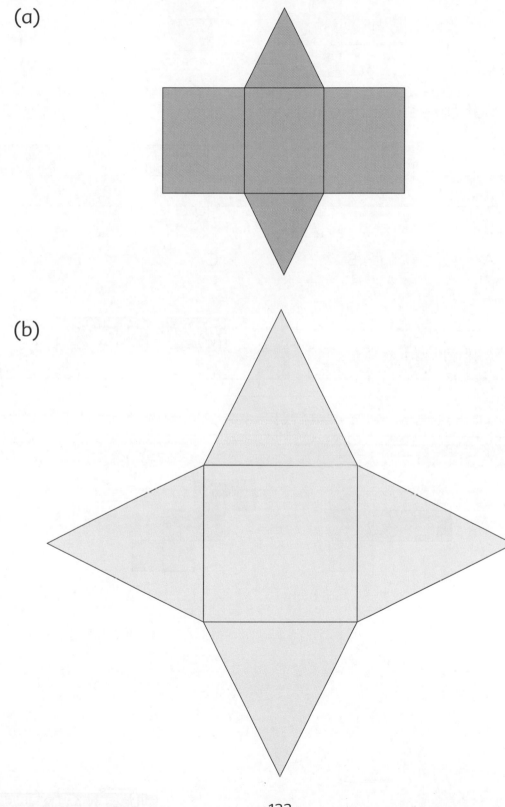

2. This is a net of a cube.

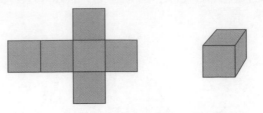

Which of these are also nets of a cube?

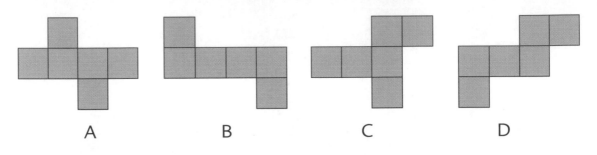

A   B   C   D

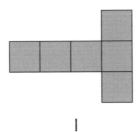

E   F   G   H

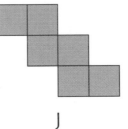

I   J

Exercise 13, pages 148-149

3. This figure shows a solid.

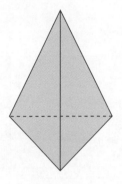

Which of the following can be a net of the solid?

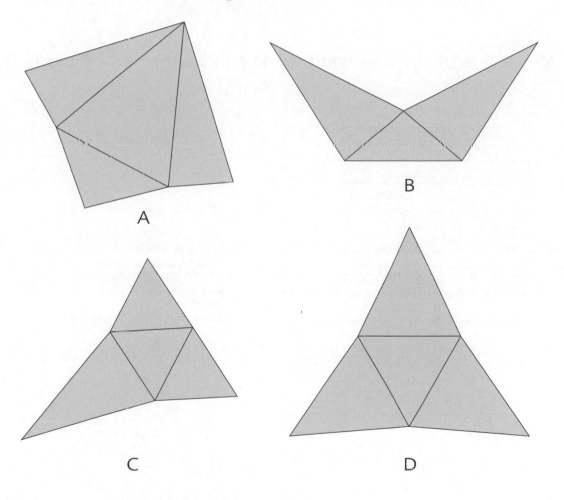

A

B

C

D

Exercise 14, pages 150-152

4. This is a net of a solid.

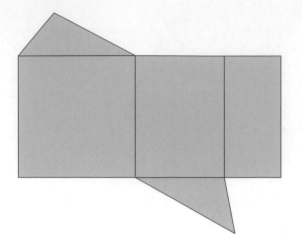

Which one of the following solids can be formed by the net?

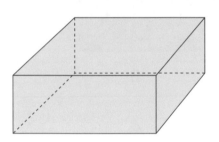

A

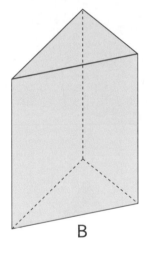

B

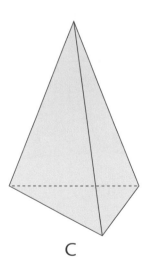

C

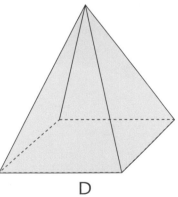

D

Exercise 15, pages 153-155

REVIEW 4

1. Write >, <, or = in place of each ⬤.

   (a) 3012 ⬤ 2998

   (b) 26,496 + 10 ⬤ 26,596

   (c) 600,100 ⬤ 600,095

   (d) 43,500 − 10 ⬤ 23,400

   (e) 5465 × 10 ⬤ 54,650

   (f) 35,000 + 10 ⬤ 350

   (g) −12 ⬤ −14

   (h) 14 ⬤ −24

2. In this figure, which line is perpendicular to line a?

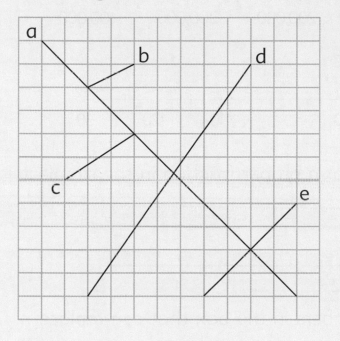

3. (a) What is point A in the picture called?
   (b) AB is called a _____ of the circle.
   (c) CD is called a _____ of the circle.
   (d) If the length of AB is 4 in., what is the length of CD?

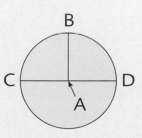

137

4. Two sides of a parallelogram have the lengths 10 cm and 8 cm. What are the lengths of the other two sides?

5. What is another name for a parallelogram with four right angles and four equal sides?

6. How many faces does the solid have? What is the name of this solid?

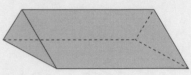

7. Write the numbers indicated by A, B, C, and D.

(a)
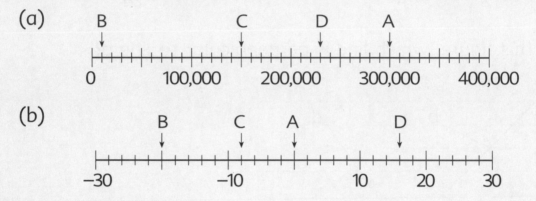

(b)

8. Write a mixed number or a proper fraction in the simplest form for A, B, C, and D.

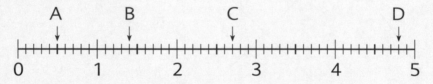

9. If $n < 5$, find all the numbers in the box that can replace n.

6	0	−3	−5	4	10

10. Find the value of each of the following expressions.
    (a) 1000 − (700 + 50)
    (b) 1000 − (700 − 50)
    (c) 6300 − (1360 − 510)
    (d) 5100 + (4800 − 2700)
    (e) (26 + 18) × 12
    (f) 23 × (53 − 45)
    (g) (135 − 30) ÷ 5
    (h) 6408 ÷ (48 − 45)

11. Find the number represented by n to make each equation true.

    (a) $\frac{4}{7} + n = 1$

    (b) $\frac{7}{9} + n = 1$

    (c) $1 - \frac{3}{10} = n$

    (d) $1 - n = \frac{1}{12}$

12. Write each of the following as a single expression and then solve it.
    (a) Subtract 100 from the product of 24 and 18.
    (b) Divide the sum of 1468 and 602 by 6.

13. Find the value of 9 ÷ 6. Give the answer as a fraction in its simplest form.

14. Which one of the following has 8 as a factor?

    $$25, \qquad 36, \qquad 48, \qquad 54$$

15. 78 is a multiple of one of the following numbers. Which is the number?

    $$6 \qquad 7 \qquad 17 \qquad 18$$

16. Arrange the numbers in increasing order.

    (a) $\frac{1}{2}, \frac{5}{12}, \frac{3}{4}, 1\frac{1}{2}$

    (b) $\frac{2}{5}, \frac{7}{10}, \frac{6}{15}, 1$

17. A rope, 40 in. long, is cut into 6 equal pieces. What is the length of each piece? Give your answer in its simplest form.

18. Sarah had $40. She used $\frac{3}{10}$ of it to buy a book. Find the cost of the book.

19. Mr. Farrell traveled $\frac{1}{3}$ of a trip on the first day.

    He traveled $\frac{4}{9}$ of the trip on the second day.

    He completed the trip on the third day.
    What fraction of the trip did he travel on the third day?

20. Miguel bought some toy cars. He gave $\frac{1}{3}$ of them to Manuel.

    If he gave 8 toy cars to Manuel, how many toy cars did Miguel buy?

21. There are 100 fruit trees in an orchard.
    $\frac{2}{5}$ of them are grapefruit trees.
    The rest of them are orange trees.
    How many orange trees are there?

22. Pauline bought a length of ribbon. She used $\frac{2}{5}$ of it to wrap a package and $\frac{1}{5}$ of it for a bow. If she used 60 in. of the ribbon, what was the length of the ribbon she bought?

5 AREA AND PERIMETER

1 Area of Rectangles

Find the area of each of the following rectangles.

Each side of the square is 1 cm long.
Its area is 1 square centimeter.

1 cm
1 cm

A square centimeter is a unit of area.
We write square centimeter like this: **cm²**.
The area of this square is 1 cm².

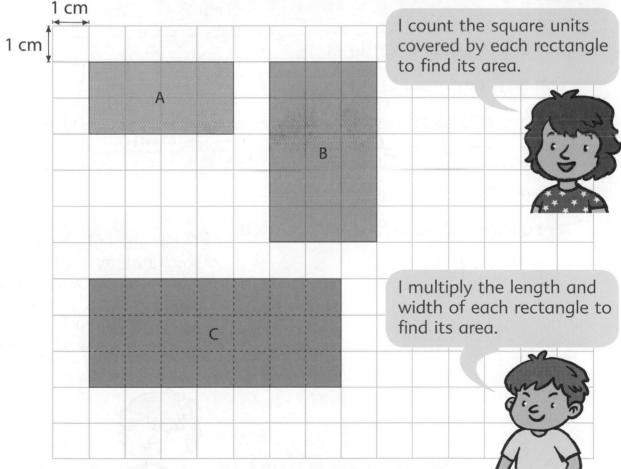

I count the square units covered by each rectangle to find its area.

I multiply the length and width of each rectangle to find its area.

Area of rectangle = length × width

We can use the symbols
A, *l* and *w* to represent
area, length and width.

The formula for area of a rectangle is
$A = l \times w$

1. Use the formula to find the
    area of this rectangle.

    Area of rectangle
    = 5 × 4 square centimeters
    = ⬜ cm²

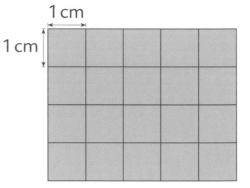

2. A square inch is also a unit of area.

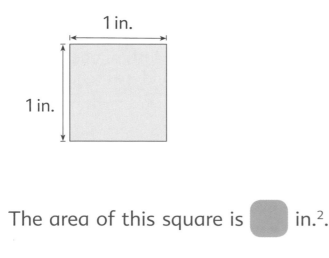

Other units of area are:
square meter (m²)
square kilometer (km²)
square foot (ft²)
square yard (yd²)
square mile (mi²)

The area of this square is ⬜ in.².

3. (a) What unit of area would you use to measure the area of a basketball court?

    (b) What unit of area would you use to measure the area of a cattle ranch?

    (c) What is the length of each side of a square yard in feet?

    (d) Is one square yard the same as three square feet since 1 yd = 3 ft?

    (e) What is the length of each side of a square kilometer in meters?

    (f) How many square centimeters is one square kilometer?

Remember?
1 m = 100 cm
1 km = 1000 m
1 ft = 12 in.
1 yd = 3 ft
1 mi = 5280 ft

4. Find the area of each of the following rectangles.

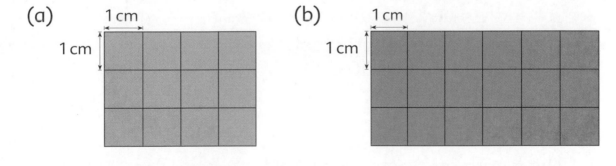

(a) 1 cm
    1 cm

(b) 1 cm
    1 cm

Exercise 1, pages 162-164

1. Find the area and the perimeter of each of the following rectangles and squares.

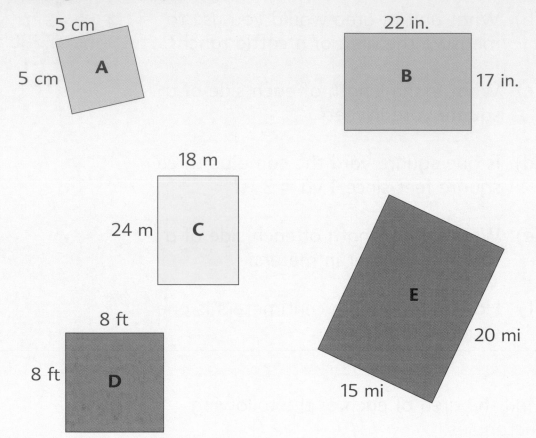

5 cm

5 cm   A

22 in.

B   17 in.

18 m

24 m   C

E   20 mi

15 mi

8 ft

8 ft   D

2. The length of the photograph is 15 cm. Its width is 10 cm. Find its area.

3. The length of a rectangular field is 85 m and its width is 10 m. Ian ran around the field once. How far did he run?

② Perimeter of Rectangles

The rectangle measures 9 cm by 5 cm.
Find its area and perimeter.

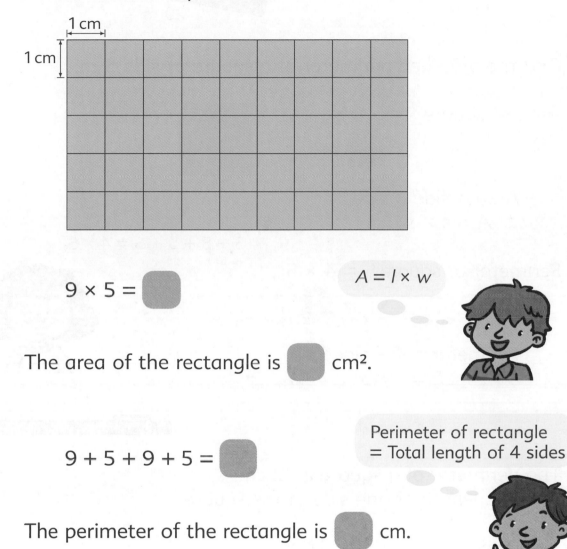

$9 \times 5 =$ ⬜

$A = l \times w$

The area of the rectangle is ⬜ cm².

$9 + 5 + 9 + 5 =$ ⬜

Perimeter of rectangle
= Total length of 4 sides

The perimeter of the rectangle is ⬜ cm.

Formula for perimeter of a rectangle:
$P = l + w + l + w$
or
$P = (2 \times l) + (2 \times w)$
or
$P = 2 \times (l + w)$

1. Find the area and perimeter of the following rectangles.

(a)

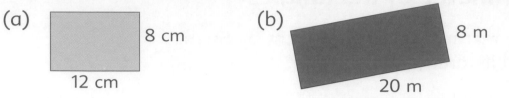

8 cm

12 cm

(b)

8 m

20 m

2. Find the area and perimeter of a square of side 5 m.

Area of square $= 5 \times 5$

$= \boxed{}$ m²

Area $=$ side $\times$ side
$A = s \times s$

5 m

$5 + 5 + 5 + 5 = 4 \times 5$

Perimeter of square $= 4 \times 5$

$= \boxed{}$ m

Perimeter $= 4 \times$ side
$P = 4 \times s$

Exercise 2, pages 165–168

3. The perimeter of a square is 12 cm.
Find the length of one side of the square.

Total length of 4 sides $= 12$ cm

$P = 4 \times s$
$s = P \div 4$
$\quad = 12 \div 4$

$\quad = \boxed{}$

?

Length of one side $= \boxed{}$ cm

4. The perimeter of a rectangle is 24 m.
   If the length of the rectangle is 8 m, find its width.

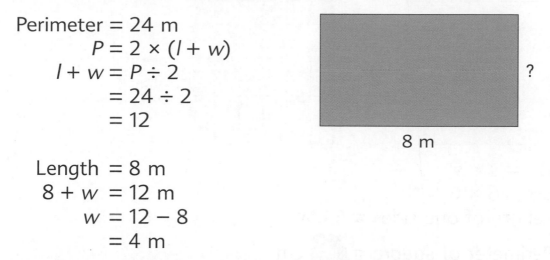

Perimeter = 24 m
$$P = 2 \times (l + w)$$
$$l + w = P \div 2$$
$$= 24 \div 2$$
$$= 12$$

Length $= 8$ m
$8 + w = 12$ m
$w = 12 - 8$
$= 4$ m

8 m

5. The rectangle and the square have the same perimeter.

   (a) Find the length of the rectangle.
   (b) Which has a bigger area, the rectangle or the square?

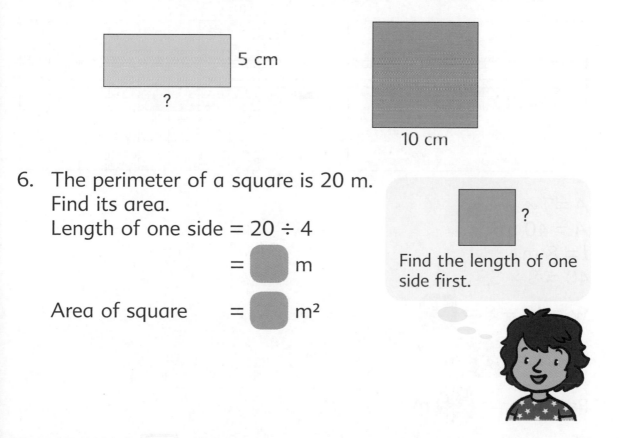

5 cm

?

10 cm

6. The perimeter of a square is 20 m.
   Find its area.
   Length of one side = 20 ÷ 4

   = ⬛ m

   Area of square = ⬛ m²

?

Find the length of one side first.

7. The area of a square is 36 cm².
    Find its perimeter.

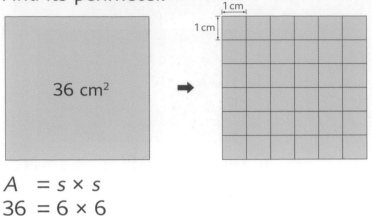

$A = s \times s$
$36 = 6 \times 6$
Length of one side $= 6$ cm

Perimeter of square = ⬜ cm

8. The area of a rectangle is 40 m².
    If the length of the rectangle is 8 m, find its width and
    perimeter.

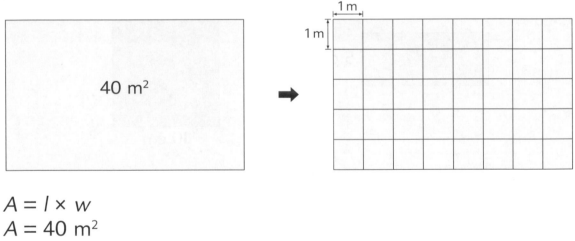

$A = l \times w$
$A = 40$ m²
$l = 8$ m
$40 = 8 \times 5$

$w = 40 \div 8 =$ ⬜

Width = ⬜ m

Perimeter = ⬜ m

148

Exercise 3, pages 169-171

1. Find the unknown side and the area of each of the following rectangles.

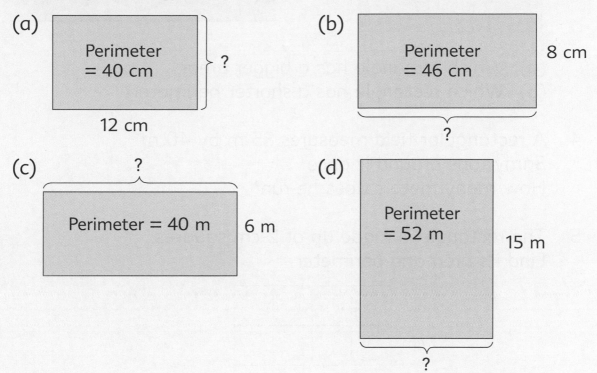

(a) Perimeter = 40 cm ? 12 cm

(b) Perimeter = 46 cm 8 cm ?

(c) ? Perimeter = 40 m 6 m

(d) Perimeter = 52 m 15 m ?

2. Find the unknown side and the perimeter of each of the following rectangles.

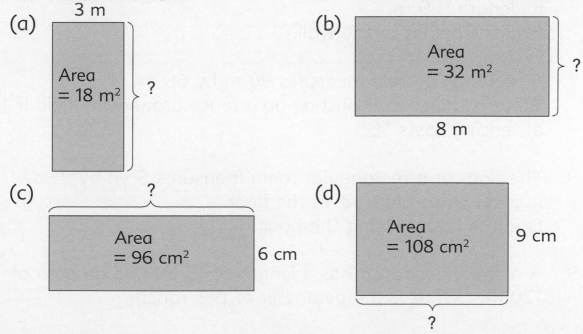

(a) 3 m Area = 18 m² ?

(b) Area = 32 m² ? 8 m

(c) ? Area = 96 cm² 6 cm

(d) Area = 108 cm² 9 cm ?

3.

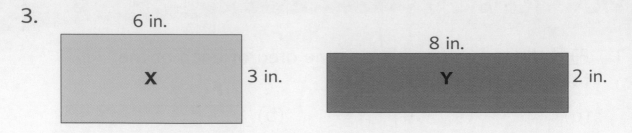

6 in.

X 3 in.

8 in.

Y 2 in.

(a) Which rectangle has a bigger area?
(b) Which rectangle has a shorter perimeter?

4. A rectangular field measures 85 m by 40 m.
Samy runs around it once.
How many meters does he run?

5. The rectangle is made up of 2-cm squares.
Find its area and perimeter.

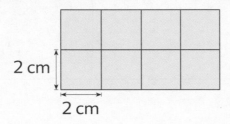

2 cm

2 cm

6. The area of a rectangular wall is 36 m².
Its length is 9 m.
Find the height of the wall.

7. A rectangular field measures 90 m by 60 m.
What is the cost of putting up a fence around the field if 1 m of fencing costs $9?

8. The floor of a rectangular room measures 5 yd by 2 yd.
It costs $6 to tile 1 yd² of the floor.
Find the cost of tiling the floor.

9. A rectangular ranch has a length of 15 mi and an area of 120 mi². What is the perimeter of this ranch?

3 Composite Figures

Each of the following figures is made up of two rectangles.
Find the area and perimeter of each figure.

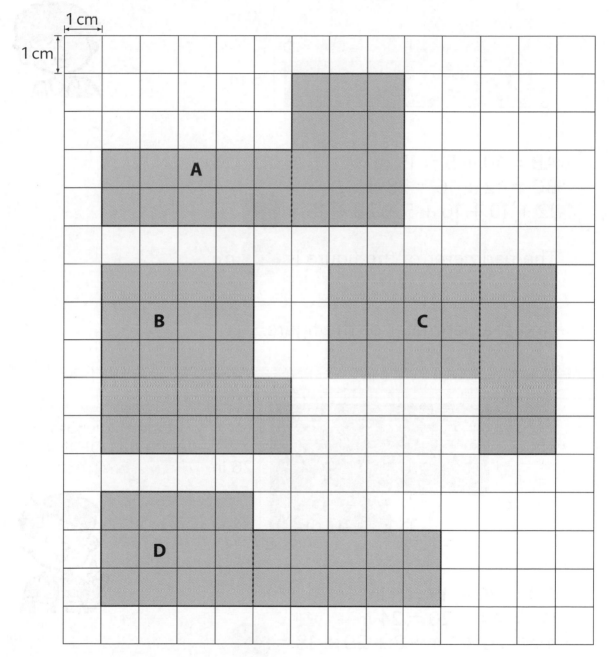

Do the figures have the same area?
Do they have the same perimeter?

1. Find the perimeter of the figure.

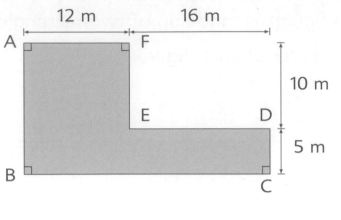

Find the lengths of AB and BC first.

AB = 10 + 5 = 15 m
BC = 12 + 16 = 28 m
12 + 10 + 16 + 5 + 28 + 15 =

The perimeter of the figure is m.

2. Find the perimeter of the figure.

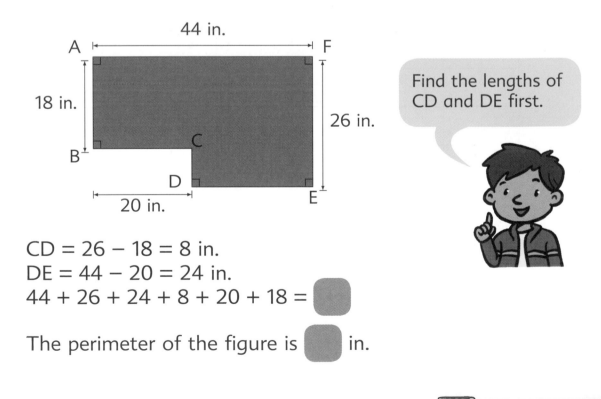

Find the lengths of CD and DE first.

CD = 26 − 18 = 8 in.
DE = 44 − 20 = 24 in.
44 + 26 + 24 + 8 + 20 + 18 =

The perimeter of the figure is in.

152

Exercise 4, pages 172-173

3. The figure is made up of two rectangles. Find its area.

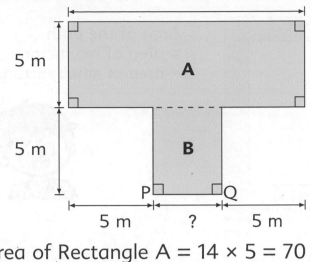

Area of the figure
= area of Rectangle A
+ area of Rectangle B

Area of Rectangle A = 14 × 5 = 70 m²
PQ = 14 − 5 − 5 = 4 m
Area of Rectangle B = 4 × 5 = 20 m²

Total area = ⬤ m²

4. The figure shows a small rectangle in a big rectangle. Find the area of the shaded part of the big rectangle.

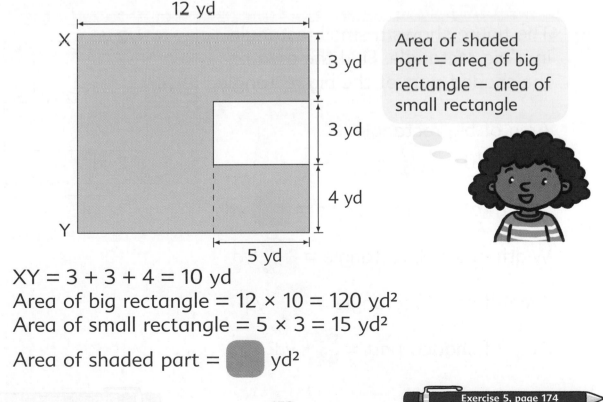

Area of shaded part = area of big rectangle − area of small rectangle

XY = 3 + 3 + 4 = 10 yd
Area of big rectangle = 12 × 10 = 120 yd²
Area of small rectangle = 5 × 3 = 15 yd²

Area of shaded part = ⬤ yd²

Exercise 5, page 174

5. The figure shows a rectangular field with a path 1 m wide around it. Find the area of the path.

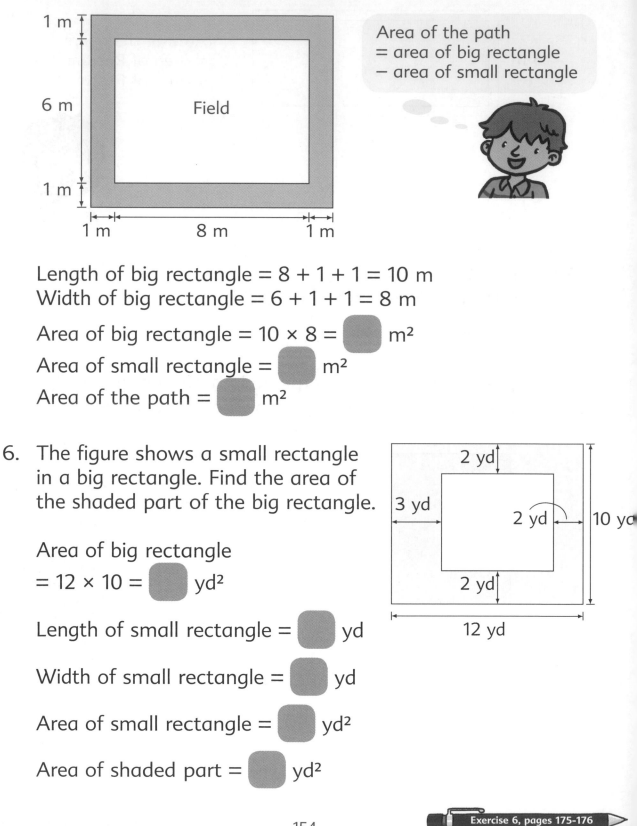

Area of the path
= area of big rectangle
− area of small rectangle

Length of big rectangle = 8 + 1 + 1 = 10 m
Width of big rectangle = 6 + 1 + 1 = 8 m

Area of big rectangle = 10 × 8 = ⬚ m²
Area of small rectangle = ⬚ m²
Area of the path = ⬚ m²

6. The figure shows a small rectangle in a big rectangle. Find the area of the shaded part of the big rectangle.

Area of big rectangle
= 12 × 10 = ⬚ yd²

Length of small rectangle = ⬚ yd

Width of small rectangle = ⬚ yd

Area of small rectangle = ⬚ yd²

Area of shaded part = ⬚ yd²

Exercise 6, pages 175-176

PRACTICE C

1. Find the area and perimeter of each figure. (All the lines meet at right angles.)

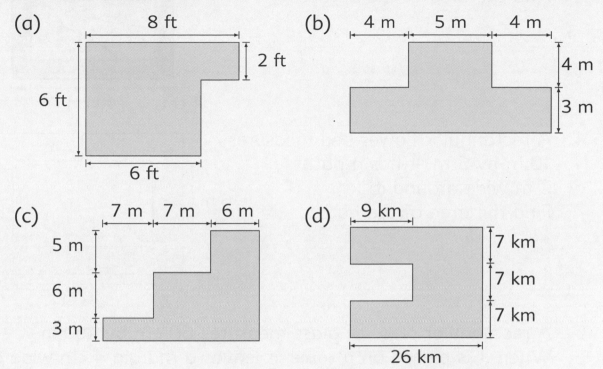

(a) 8 ft, 2 ft, 6 ft, 6 ft

(b) 4 m, 5 m, 4 m, 4 m, 3 m

(c) 7 m, 7 m, 6 m, 5 m, 6 m, 3 m

(d) 9 km, 7 km, 7 km, 7 km, 26 km

2. Find the shaded area of each rectangle. (All the lines meet at right angles.)

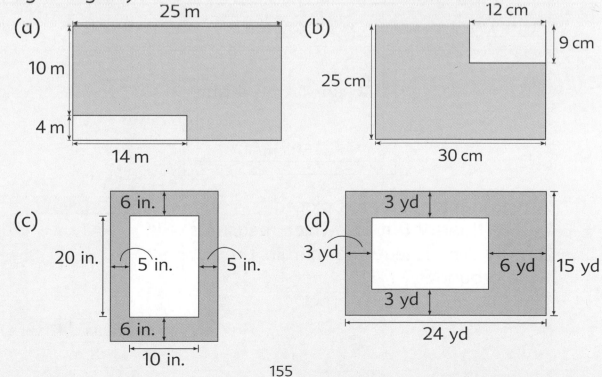

(a) 25 m, 10 m, 4 m, 14 m

(b) 12 cm, 9 cm, 25 cm, 30 cm

(c) 6 in., 20 in., 5 in., 5 in., 6 in., 10 in.

(d) 3 yd, 3 yd, 6 yd, 15 yd, 3 yd, 24 yd

155

3. The border around a square painting
    is 4 cm wide. Each side of the painting
    is 40 cm long.
    Find the area of the border.

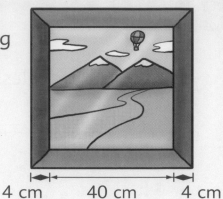

4 cm   40 cm   4 cm

4. A rectangular flower-bed measures
    10 m by 6 m. It has a path
    2 m wide around it.
    Find the area of the path.

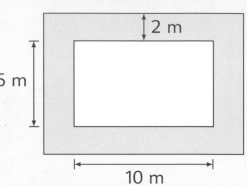

5. A rectangular piece of glass measures 60 cm by 46 cm.
    When it is placed on a table, it leaves a margin 4 cm wide all
    around it. What is the area of the table-top **not** covered by
    the glass?

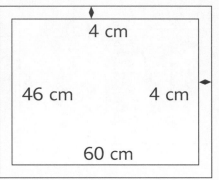

4 cm

46 cm   4 cm

60 cm

6. A rectangular carpet is placed
    on the floor of a room which measures
    8 m by 7 m. It leaves a margin 1 m
    wide around it.
    Find the area of the carpet.

1 m   1 m   1 m   7 m

1 m

8 m

1. Estimate and then multiply.
    (a) 39 × 19   (b) 48 × 22   (c) 99 × 4
    (d) 208 × 31   (e) 512 × 28   (f) 198 × 6

2. The product of two numbers is 108.
    If one of the numbers is 6, what is the other number?

3. Name three equivalent fractions for each of these fractions.
    (a) $\frac{2}{3}$ (b) $\frac{1}{5}$ (c) $\frac{9}{12}$

4. Arrange the numbers in increasing order.
    (a) $\frac{3}{4}, \frac{2}{3}, \frac{5}{6}$ (b) $\frac{7}{4}, 1\frac{7}{10}, 2$

5. Write each fraction in its simplest form.
    (a) $\frac{6}{8}$ (b) $\frac{18}{24}$ (c) $\frac{20}{50}$

6. Write >, <, or = in place of each ◯.
    (a) $\frac{9}{10}$ ◯ $\frac{3}{4}$ (b) $1\frac{1}{4}$ ◯ $\frac{10}{8}$ (c) $1\frac{2}{3}$ ◯ $\frac{3}{2}$

7. Write the next three numbers in the following regular number pattern.
    20, 15, 10, 5, ▢ , ▢ , ▢

8. List the prime numbers between 5 and 15.

9. Arrange these numbers in increasing order.
    6,   −6,   3,   0,   −11,   −2,   7

10. How many faces does each of the following have?
    (a) cube
    (b) rectangular prism
    (c) triangular prism
    (d) rectangular pyramid
    (e) triangular pyramid
    (f) cylinder

11. For each of the following, say whether the statement is
    always true, sometimes true, or never true for rhombuses.

    Two pairs of opposite sides are parallel.
    Opposite sides are of the same length.
    All four sides are of the same length.
    All four angles are right angles.

12. Find the missing numbers.

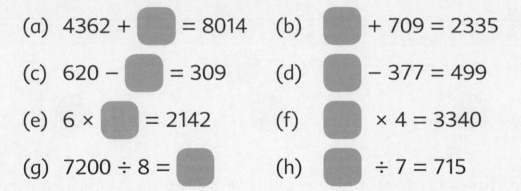

    (a) 4362 + ▢ = 8014   (b) ▢ + 709 = 2335

    (c) 620 − ▢ = 309   (d) ▢ − 377 = 499

    (e) 6 × ▢ = 2142   (f) ▢ × 4 = 3340

    (g) 7200 ÷ 8 = ▢   (h) ▢ ÷ 7 = 715

13. Write a single expression that you could use to find the
    answer to the following problem, and then solve it.
    Martin has $1 and wants to buy 3 candy bars. Each candy
    bar costs a quarter. How much change will he get?

14. Find the product of 348 and 39.

15. Susan saved $70 in 5 weeks. If she saved an equal amount each week, how much would she save in 8 weeks?

16. Mrs. Wang cuts 9 m of ribbon equally into 4 parts. How long is each part?

17. O is the center of the circle. What kind of triangle is Triangle OSR?

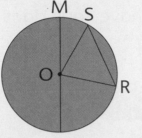

18. Which of the following are nets of a cube?

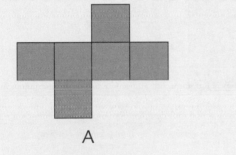

A

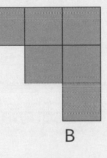

B

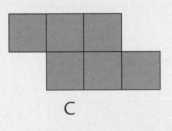

C

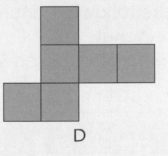

D

19.

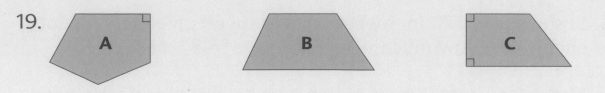

(a) Which figures have perpendicular lines?
(b) Which figures have parallel lines?
(c) Which figure has both perpendicular and parallel lines?

20. Which of the following figures have four right angles?
    Which is a square?

21. Find the length and perimeter of the rectangle.

Area = 78 m²   6 m

22. The perimeter of a square is 48 cm.
    Find its area.

23. Each of the following figures shows a small rectangle
    in a big rectangle.
    Find the area of the shaded part of each figure.

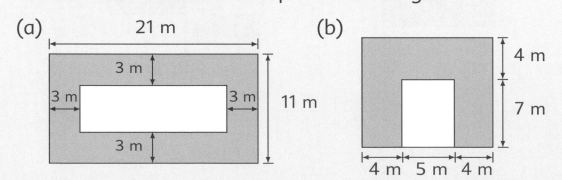

(a) 21 m   3 m   3 m   3 m   3 m   11 m

(b) 4 m   7 m   4 m   5 m   4 m

24. Find the area and perimeter of each figure. (All lines meet at right angles.)

(a)

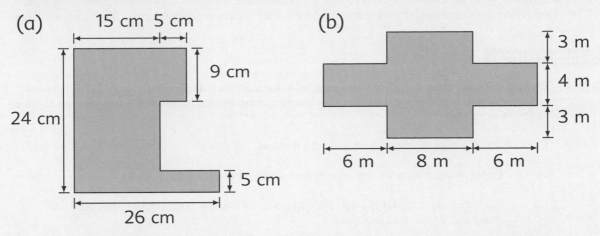

(b)

25. Seth used $4\frac{2}{5}$ yd of rope to pitch a tent. Roger used $\frac{3}{10}$ yd less rope to pitch another tent. How many yards of rope did they use altogether?

26. Twelve pieces of ribbon, each 75 in. long, are cut from a length of ribbon 1250 in. long. What is the length of the remaining piece of ribbon?

27. 45 people took part in a swimming competition. The number of people who took part in a walkathon was 12 times the number of people who took part in the swimming competition. How many more people took part in the walkathon than in the swimming competition?

28. Rolando imported 138 boxes of mangoes. There were 24 mangoes in each box. He reserved 72 mangoes for his friends and sold the rest to 3 customers. If each customer bought an equal number of mangoes, how many mangoes did each customer buy?

Review 5, pages 177-184

Grade Four Mathematics Content Standards

By the end of grade four, students understand large numbers and addition, subtraction, multiplication, and division of whole numbers. They describe and compare simple fractions and decimals. They understand the properties of, and the relationships between, plane geometric figures. They collect, represent, and analyze data to answer questions.

Number Sense

1.0 **Students understand the place value of whole numbers and decimals to two decimal places and how whole numbers and decimals relate to simple fractions. Students use the concepts of negative numbers:**

1.1 Read and write whole numbers in the millions.

1.2 Order and compare whole numbers and decimals to two decimal places.

1.3 Round whole numbers through the millions to the nearest ten, hundred, thousand, ten thousand, or hundred thousand.

1.4 Decide when a rounded solution is called for and explain why such a solution may be appropriate.

1.5 Explain different interpretations of fractions, for example, parts of a whole, parts of a set, and division of whole numbers by whole numbers; explain equivalence of fractions (see Standard 4.0).

1.6 Write tenths and hundredths in decimal and fraction notations and know the fraction and decimal equivalents for halves and fourths (e.g., ½ = 0.5 or 0.50; 7/4 = 1¾ = 1.75).

1.7 Write the fraction represented by a drawing of parts of a figure; represent a given fraction by using drawings; and relate a fraction to a simple decimal on a number line.

1.8 Use concepts of negative numbers (e.g., on a number line, in counting, in temperature, in "owing").

1.9 Identify on a number line the relative position of positive fractions, positive mixed numbers, and positive decimals to two decimal places.

2.0 **Students extend their use and understanding of whole numbers to the addition and subtraction of simple decimals:**

2.1 Estimate and compute the sum or difference of whole numbers and positive decimals to two places.

2.2 Round two-place decimals to one decimal or to the nearest whole number and judge the reasonableness of the rounded answer.

3.0 **Students solve problems involving addition, subtraction, multiplication, and division of whole numbers and understand the relationships among the operations:**

3.1 Demonstrate an understanding of, and the ability to use, standard algorithms for the addition and subtraction of multidigit numbers.

3.2 Demonstrate an understanding of, and the ability to use, standard algorithms for multiplying a multidigit number by a two-digit number and for dividing a multidigit number by a one-digit number; use relationships between them to simplify computations and to check results.

3.3   Solve problems involving multiplication of multidigit numbers by two-digit numbers.

3.4   Solve problems involving division of multidigit numbers by one-digit numbers.

4.0   Students know how to factor small whole numbers:

4.1   Understand that many whole numbers break down in different ways (e.g., $12 = 4 \times 3 = 2 \times 6 = 2 \times 2 \times 3$).

4.2   Know that numbers such as 2, 3, 5, 7, and 11 do not have any factors except 1 and themselves and that such numbers are called prime numbers.

Algebra and Functions

1.0   Students use and interpret variables, mathematical symbols, and properties to write and simplify expressions and sentences:

1.1   Use letters, boxes, or other symbols to stand for any number in simple expressions or equations (e.g., demonstrate an understanding and the use of the concept of a variable).

1.2   Interpret and evaluate mathematical expressions that now use parentheses.

1.3   Use parentheses to indicate which operation to perform first when writing expressions containing more than two terms and different operations.

1.4   Use and interpret formulas (e.g., area = length $\times$ width or $A = lw$) to answer questions about quantities and their relationships.

1.5   Understand that an equation such as $y = 3x + 5$ is a prescription for determining a second number when a first number is given.

2.0   Students know how to manipulate equations:

2.1   Know and understand that equals added to equals are equal.

2.2   Know and understand that equals multiplied by equals are equal.

Measurement and Geometry

1.0   Students understand perimeter and area:

1.1   Measure the area of rectangular shapes by using appropriate units, such as square centimeter (cm^2), square meter (m^2), square kilometer (km^2), square inch ($in.^2$), square yard ($yd.^2$), or square mile ($mi.^2$).

1.2   Recognize that rectangles that have the same area can have different perimeters.

1.3   Understand that rectangles that have the same perimeter can have different areas.

1.4   Understand and use formulas to solve problems involving perimeters and areas of rectangles and squares. Use those formulas to find the areas of more complex figures by dividing the figures into basic shapes.

2.0 Students use two-dimensional coordinate grids to represent points and graph lines and simple figures:

2.1   Draw the points corresponding to linear relationships on graph paper (e.g., draw 10 points on the graph of the equation $y = 3x$ and connect them by using a straight line).

2.2   Understand that the length of a horizontal line segment equals the difference of the x-coordinates.

2.3   Understand that the length of a vertical line segment equals the difference of the y-coordinates.

3.0 Students demonstrate an understanding of plane and solid geometric objects and use this knowledge to show relationships and solve problems:

3.1   Identify lines that are parallel and perpendicular. (Teachers are advised to introduce the terms intersecting lines and nonintersecting lines when dealing with this standard.)

3.2   Identify the radius and diameter of a circle.

3.3   Identify congruent figures.

3.4   Identify figures that have bilateral and rotational symmetry.

3.5   Know the definitions of a right angle, an acute angle, and an obtuse angle. Understand that 90°, 180°, 270°, and 360° are associated, respectively, with ¼, ½, ¾ and full turns.

3.6   Visualize, describe, and make models of geometric solids (e.g., prisms, pyramids) in terms of the number and shape of faces, edges, and vertices; interpret two-dimensional representations of three-dimensional objects; and draw patterns (of faces) for a solid that, when cut and folded, will make a model of the solid.

3.7   Know the definitions of different triangles (e.g., equilateral, isosceles, scalene) and identify their attributes.

3.8   Know the definition of different quadrilaterals (e.g., rhombus, square, rectangle, parallelogram, trapezoid).

Statistics, Data Analysis, and Probability

1.0 Students organize, represent, and interpret numerical and categorical data and clearly communicate their findings:

1.1   Formulate survey questions; systematically collect and represent data on a number line; and coordinate graphs, tables, and charts.

1.2   Identify the mode(s) for sets of categorical data and the mode(s), median, and any apparent outliers for numerical data sets.

1.3   Interpret one- and two-variable data graphs to answer questions about a situation.

2.0   Students make predictions for simple probability situations:

    2.1   Represent all possible outcomes for a simple probability situation in an organized way (e.g., tables, grids, tree diagrams).

    2.2   Express outcomes of experimental probability situations verbally and numerically (e.g., 3 out of 4; ¾).

Mathematical Reasoning

1.0   Students make decisions about how to approach problems:

    1.1   Analyze problems by identifying relationships, distinguishing relevant from irrelevant information, sequencing and prioritizing information, and observing patterns.

    1.2   Determine when and how to break a problem into simpler parts.

2.0   Students use strategies, skills, and concepts in finding solutions:

    2.1   Use estimation to verify the reasonableness of calculated results.

    2.2   Apply strategies and results from simpler problems to more complex problems.

    2.3   Use a variety of methods, such as words, numbers, symbols, charts, graphs, tables, diagrams, and models, to explain mathematical reasoning.

    2.4   Express the solution clearly and logically by using the appropriate mathematical notation and terms and clear language; support solutions with evidence in both verbal and symbolic work.

    2.5   Indicate the relative advantages of exact and approximate solutions to problems and give answers to a specified degree of accuracy.

    2.6   Make precise calculations and check the validity of the results from the context of the problem.

3.0   Students move beyond a particular problem by generalizing to other situations:

    3.1   Evaluate the reasonableness of the solution in the context of the original situation.

    3.2   Note the method of deriving the solution and demonstrate a conceptual understanding of the derivation by solving similar problems.

    3.3   Develop generalizations of the results obtained and apply them in other circumstances.

GLOSSARY

Word	Meaning
acute angle	An **acute** angle is an angle that is smaller than a right angle. 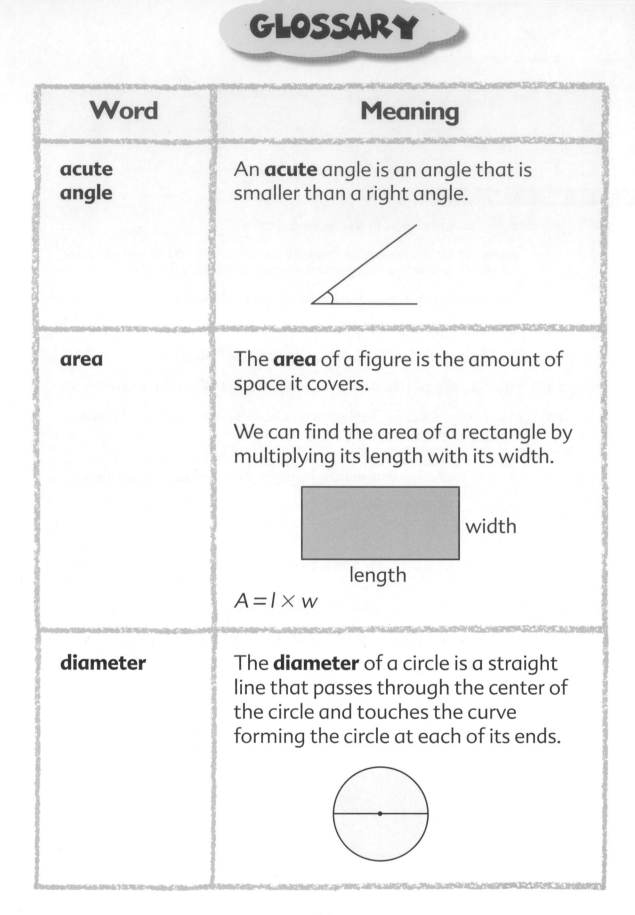
area	The **area** of a figure is the amount of space it covers. We can find the area of a rectangle by multiplying its length with its width. width length $A = l \times w$
diameter	The **diameter** of a circle is a straight line that passes through the center of the circle and touches the curve forming the circle at each of its ends.

Word	Meaning
equivalent fractions	**Equivalent fractions** are fractions that are equal in value. $\dfrac{1}{3} = \dfrac{2}{6} = \dfrac{3}{9}$
improper fractions	An **improper fraction** is a fraction that is equal to or greater than 1. $\dfrac{3}{3}, \quad \dfrac{4}{3}, \quad \dfrac{5}{3}$
multiples	The first 5 **multiples** of 3 are 3, 6, 9, 12 and 15.
negative numbers	Numbers that are on the left of the number line are called **negative numbers**.
net	A figure that can be folded to form a solid is called a **net** of the solid.

Word	Meaning
obtuse angle	An **obtuse angle** is an angle that is greater than a right angle but less than two right angles. 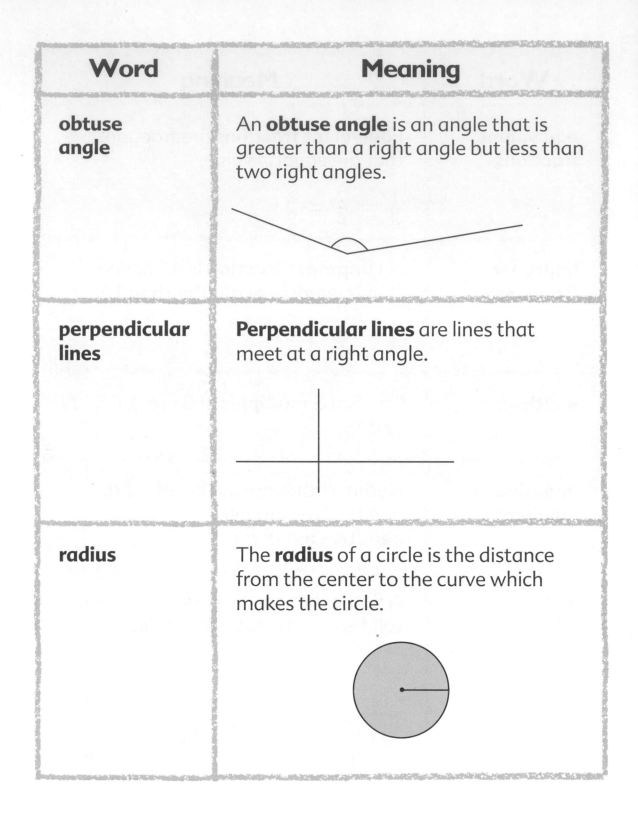
perpendicular lines	**Perpendicular lines** are lines that meet at a right angle.
radius	The **radius** of a circle is the distance from the center to the curve which makes the circle.

Index

Blank